D0082647

MAN AND THE ENVIRONMENT

MAN AND THE ENVIRONMENT

A Study of St Symeon the New Theologian

by

Anestis G. Keselopoulos

translated by
Elizabeth Theokritoff

ST VLADIMIR'S SEMINARY PRESS
CRESTWOOD, NEW YORK
2001

Library of Congress Cataloging-in-Publication Data
Keselopoulos, Anestes G.

[Anthropos kai physiko perivallon. English]

Man and the environment: a study of St. Symeon the New Theologian /
by Anestis G. Keselopoulos; translated by Elizabeth Theokritoff.

p. cm.

Includes bibliographical references.

ISBN 0-88141-221-X (alk. paper)

1. Symeon, the New Theologian, Saint, 949-1022—Views on man and environment. 2. Human ecology—Religious aspects—Christianity. I. Title
BX395.S9 K4713 2001
261.8'362'092—dc21

00-067364

Copyright © 2001

ST VLADIMIR'S SEMINARY PRESS
575 Scarsdale Rd., Crestwood, NY 10707
1-800-204-2665

A translation of *Anthropos kai Physiko Perivallon: Spoudi ston Agio
Symeon to Neo Theologo* (1st edition, Athens: Domos, 1979)

ISBN 0-88141-221-X

All Rights Reserved

PRINTED IN THE UNITED STATES OF AMERICA

For my son Dimitris,
who gave me my "alternative education" in the
renewal of the world.

Contents

FOREWORD

The crisis in man's relationship with his natural environment is of particular concern to the modern world. The pollution of rivers and seas, atmospheric pollution, the destruction of natural resources, the accumulation of radioactive waste and so many other phenomena bear witness to the existence of an acute, disquieting ecological crisis, and anxiety is often expressed about this.

This anxiety is commonly reflected in report after report from international organizations, or the establishment of a "year of the environment," or endless discussions among ecologists who talk about the crisis and try to find solutions to it. But it is particularly curious that while we are faced with phenomena which testify to the violation of nature by man, in so many cases there is not the slightest suspicion that the crisis is not only scientific, but first and foremost spiritual. Hence the solutions proposed range from the search for some "better technology" to the romantic "back to nature" approach.

Orthodox patristic thought and theology did not involve itself in such tugs-of-war, because it saw nature as the creation and work of God. The relationship between man and the environment, which it puts forward as alone being true and salutary, is one that passes through man's relationship and communion with God. The teaching of St Symeon the New Theologian on this subject, which is the topic of this study, is especially revealing, because it takes as its starting point the authentic theology, anthropology and cosmology which he professes.

I should like to take this opportunity to express my warm thanks to Professor Georgios Mantzaridis for the encouragement he has given me to work on this topic and also for his invaluable advice and suggestions.

Introduction

Man lives in coexistence and direct relationship with his environment and creation in general. This coexistence and the quality of this relationship sets its mark on the quality of his life. Holy Scripture, the Fathers and the whole of the Church's liturgical tradition and life refer frequently to man's relationship with creation, underlining the necessity of harmony in this relationship. They also indicate ways for man and nature to work together, opening up paths that man must follow in order to arrive with creation at his ultimate goal, salvation.

According to the patristic tradition, the coexistence of man and nature is placed on the level of friendly relations, not of conflict or oppression of the one by the other. Correspondingly, in the Church's worship and liturgical life there is a harmony and cohesion between the sensible and intelligible elements in creation. This vision does not permit a polarized division or a contrast between the sensible and intelligible worlds, between matter and spirit. These two elements make up created reality. And although they can be distinguished, they form between them a harmonious synthesis. Neither the material nor the spiritual can be looked at independently of the Church. Furthermore, modern philosophy and science generally follow this approach, rejecting conflicts and contrasts between matter and spirit and trying to see and interpret the world and man on the basis of unity and interdependence.

Any conflicts between dualistic elements fragment the unity of the world and of life which the Church accepts and serves. The teaching of the Fathers on this point was revolutionary in character and was able to integrate a world of manifold idols into the natural and historical reality. The Orthodox tradition more generally came and took up apparently disparate elements of the world, recast various aspects of life, and proclaimed through her daily practice that spiritual and material-bodily functions are not in a state of dualistic conflict, but in a relationship of complementarity. The Church permeates historical, natural and intelligible reality and grafts it into herself, embracing the whole of creation. This is why she did not simply refuse to accept any depreciation of the material and sensible element that was attempted in the name of the "spiritual life" of the faithful or of some "more spiritual" theology; she fought it systematically through Councils.

The monophysite and iconoclast heresies were hostile to the sensible and human dimension; they gave autonomy to the spiritual element and above all overlooked the significance of the human body. From the theology of the Fathers and the liturgical texts of the Church—particularly the *Euchologion* or *Trebnik*[1]—one can see the attitude of the Church towards the material world and the environment. This attitude is not simply positive, but above all one that takes up the world and transfigures it. Even more importantly, the Eucharist—the sovereign element of the Church's life, is an affirmation of the worth of materiality, raising it to participation in the true Life which is Christ. Right belief in the incarnate Word of God also gives the Church a proper position and orientation vis-à-vis matter. Thus she does not reject matter like the Manicheans, nor worship it like the pagans, nor regard it as theologically indifferent, but confesses her faith through the mouth of St John of Damascus when he says: "I worship the Creator of matter who became matter for my sake, who willed to take His abode in matter; who worked out my salvation through

---

1   Translator's note: The "Book of Needs," containing occasional services, prayers and blessings.

matter. Never will I cease honoring the matter which wrought my salvation! I honor it, but not as God... [but] because God has filled it with His grace and power."[2]

On the other hand, creation communes with God. Every created thing presupposes God's love and is present in the Mind of God. Yet this communion is crowned and consummated in the interpersonal relationships of rational beings. When communication between humans and God is removed, relations between them are disrupted, and the consequence is misuse of creation and violation of the environment. Only when man has a relationship with God and creation which is in accordance with nature can we speak of true communion and the attainment of salvation ("salvation" essentially meaning that man and creation become safe, sound, whole), since keeping to what is in accordance with nature is regarded as a precondition for the increase by grace in the community of rational beings. And when we talk about creation, nature and history, in the final analysis we mean the life of a particular community of people in relation to God and to every element in creation.

Here it should be noted that this study also aims to be self-critical; critical not only of the thoroughly consumerist character of some "Christian" societies, but also of the excesses upheld at times by Christian idealism, which certainly do not lead to a positive vision of material creation and a real appreciation of its worth. For it is only Orthodox cosmology, far removed as it is from the eccentricities of any form of magic or idolatry or autonomous nature worship, that is able through the authenticity of its tradition to offer a positive valuation and utilization of the material being of the world.

The event of the Transfiguration underlines the importance of the human body. The Transfiguration is a consummate affirmation

2   *On the Divine Images* I.16, PG 94.1300AB; tr. David Anderson, St John of Damascus: *On the Divine Images* (Crestwood, 1980), p. 23.

of the worth of the sensible and of matter. When Christ was transfigured on Mount Tabor, His divine glory was manifested in His body and the Disciples saw Him—as far as they were able—with their material eyes. Because of the divine Incarnation, the glory of the Godhead was manifested as the glory and beauty of the body, the glory and beauty of creation which as a "vessel" receives the divine energy.[3] As the glory of Christ is not the glory of the divine nature only but also of the human nature, so there is an analogy with what happens regarding the glory of the saints. Their transfiguration does not involve only the soul but also the body, which "is deified together with the soul according to the participation in deification appropriate to it."[4]

The ultimate affirmation of the human body is evidenced in the Orthodox Church with the honor paid to holy relics, which stems directly from her faith and theology. As St Gregory Palamas notes, just as Christ's divinity did not abandon His deified human body during His three-day burial and Resurrection, even so the Grace of God which deifies the saints does not abandon their bodies after their biological death.[5]

Belief in the ultimate transfiguration and renewal of the world—about which so much is said in Scripture and the Church Fathers—offers a real possibility for extending the theology of holy relics to the rest of creation. At the Second Coming, it is not only the bodies of the righteous that will be raised; the whole of material creation will be renewed as well. This is why, during this period of waiting for the Last Day, the Church venerates with honor not only the relics of the saints, but also their clothes, the

---

3 St John of Damascus, *On the Divine Images* 3.34, PG 94.1353B; tr. David Anderson, *On the Divine Images* (Crestwood, 1980), p. 86: "I honor and venerate all God's holy temples, and everything where God's name is found, not for their own sake, but because they are vessels of divine power."

4 Maximus the Confessor, *Gnostic Chapters* 2.8, PG 90.1168A.

5 See *A New Testament Decalogue*, PG 150.1093A; ET *Philokalia* IV (tr. G.E.H. Palmer, Philip Sherrard and Kallistos Ware, London, 1995), p. 325.

places where they lived, the things they used and anything else connected with them. It is not only the bodies of the saints that are sanctified; the material objects that surround them also participate in sanctification. At the Last Day, inanimate objects too will be transfigured, as the human body will.

The doctrine of the transfiguration of the world—which takes its starting point from Christ's coming and His presence in this world—and of the body's participation in the life of grace, received its consummate formulation and expression in the writings of the Fathers. St Gregory Palamas, after a challenge by his opponents, spoke of the worth of matter, the place of the body in the experience of prayer and the transfiguration of the body. "The spiritual delight which comes upon the body from the intellect,"[6] he writes, "is itself in no way corrupted by its communion with the body, but transforms the body and makes it spiritual." And he emphasizes that "it is not the soul alone that receives the surety of good things to come, but also the body which completes with it the course to these good things of the Gospel."[7]

The iconography of the Orthodox Church stresses the close bond between man and creation. In its various presentations of themes mainly from the Old and New Testaments, it depicts the harmony and peace of creation, always in a relationship of perfect concord with man. The fact that man, as the crown of creation, is always put in the foreground while the rest of creation is arranged as a background, not only shows man's dominant position in creation but also the responsibility he has for rightly coexisting with it properly. One of the themes in Byzantine iconography "recounts" in summary the two creation stories in Genesis that refer to man's relationship with creation. Another theme arises out

6 Translator's note: The noun "intellect" is used throughout in the sense of the spiritual intellect or *nous;* not the discursive reason, but the faculty through which man is able directly to apprehend divine truth.

7 *In Defence of the Holy Hesychasts* 1.3.5, Writings of St Gregory Palamas, ed. P. Chrestou, vol. 1 (Thessaloniki, 1962), p. 413.

of the prophecy of Isaiah (Is 11:6-9) in which the prophet sees the vision of a future peace in the world, without any discord between man and creation or within creation itself. When later on Christian art becomes historical and narrative, once again creation is depicted schematically alongside man, in order to stress that man and creation go hand in hand towards their ultimate renewal and salvation.[8] Thus the icon, a sign of the triumph of God's grace over the rebellious elements which obscure and darken matter, creation, and also the heart of man, heralds the restoration to creation of its true order.

St Symeon is one of the few Fathers of the Church who has been given the title of "Theologian." This is because in St Symeon the Orthodox Tradition has always seen a great teacher and theologian of Christian faith and life. His name was the center of considerable controversy among his contemporaries, at least according to the *Life* of him written by his disciple Nikitas Stethatos, a fine text which provides much important information about his life and work.[9] Much more information for a inner biography of the Saint is provided by his own works, especially the *Hymns of Divine Love*.[10] These writings reveal the spiritual state and theological climate of the period in which he lived (tenth to eleventh centuries), a period when spiritual life was in danger of being formalized and reduced to routine and stagnation. It seemed at that time that "the 'newness' of the Gospel had been forgotten, the ever new, dynamic and grace-filled life in Christ through the grace of the Holy Spirit. In the same way,

8   I. Galanis, "The New Testament Foundation for the relations between Man and Creation in the Church's Worship," (in Greek), in *Epistimoniki Epeteris tis Theologikis Scholis, Volume in Honor of Professor Emeritus Konstantinos Kalokyris* (Thessaloniki, 1985), pp. 399-400.

9   Edited by P. Hausherr in the series *Orientalia Christiana* no. 45 (Rome, 1928), pp. 1-228.

10   The 58 *Hymns* of Symeon have been edited in the series "Sources Chrétiennes," Vols. 156, 174 and 196. They are translated in G. Maloney, *Hymns of Divine Love* (Denville, New Jersey). See further in the bibliography.

theology at that time was presented as a sterile preservation or formal repetition of the Tradition, not vivified by personal experience in the Church and spiritual witness."[11]

Byzantium had nevertheless retained a memorial and expression of some Tradition and life—the Byzantine art of earlier times, especially the architecture. The ethos and stance represented by this art was for St Symeon a personal study in the possibilities offered by physical matter and creation. In the world of Byzantine art we have not only a personal use of the construction material, but also a personal dialogue with the material. We have the personal encounter and relationship between man and the *logos*, the "inner principle" of God's love and wisdom which is revealed in material creation. This dialogue, incarnate in every Byzantine creation, gave the measure of the truth of the whole natural world as communion and Church and taught the Byzantines how material creation is "given shape" and how non-rational and dumb creation is "made word," *logos*.

St Symeon the New Theologian is often presented as a mystic who spoke exclusively about exalted spiritual states such as dispassion and the vision of light and deification, without showing a corresponding interest in the ways and means leading to these states—in the ascetic life and the daily struggle against the passions, which were the principle subjects discussed by the Fathers before him. What is more, no emphasis at all has been given to his teaching on man's relationship with the world and the environment. But although the particular stress on conscious mystical experience is the special characteristic of this holy Father, we should not overlook that teaching of his which relates not only to the ascetic dimension, but also to the social dimension of human life. The ascetic struggle holds a significant and fundamental place in his works, even though this aspect of his writing

11 See Hieromonk [now Metropolitan] Athanasius Jevtic, *Foreword* to the Greek edition of Archbishop Basil Krivocheine, *In the Light of Christ* (Thessaloniki, 1983), p. 7.

gives the impression of being less original and follows the line already laid down by Fathers before him.[12] The particular hallmark of his teaching is his insistent effort not to separate the ascetic struggle from the mystical life.

Here we must also underline that the spiritual life which St Symeon talks about in his writings is not exclusively the concern of monks; what he has to say is directed to every human being, monastic or not. Hence he criticizes certain people whom the monks of his day considered "famous and glorious for their virtue"[13] because they did not have a true sense of spiritual life and were trying to substitute a barren and superficial asceticism meant for themselves alone. Despite his monastic state and radical renunciation of the world, his interests are not confined to the concerns of his monastery, but extend to the life of lay people and the community at large. On the basis of the Gospel teaching, he is sharply critical of the social order of his day which represented misuse of creation and material luxury. Ten centuries before the present ecological impasse, he points out the connection of environmental problems with the social and economic problem in our use of the world and of material goods. The ecological crisis is an expression and a generalization of the social problem. St Symeon notes man's tendency to tyrannize his social and his natural environment. This tendency to possess and misuse, which in the first place created the social problem, has now led to the ecological crisis. Especially in his *Catechetical Discourses*, he lashes out against private property—particularly of land, and also more generally of wealth—as a source of social inequality and suffering among humans.[14] What is most

12 See W. Völker, *Praxis und Theoria bei Symeon dem Neuen Theologen. Ein Beitrag zur byzantinischen Mystik* (Wiesbaden, 1974), p. 485. W. Völker's contribution lies in the fact that with this work, he gave St Symeon's ascetic teaching its rightful place and made clear its affinity with the corresponding teaching of the patristic tradition before him.

13 *Catechetical Discourses* 4, SC 96, p. 314.

14 *Catechetical Orations* 9, SC 104, pp. 110-112.

important, he does not isolate these problems, but connects them with man's overriding problem, which is a false relationship with God. The oppressive and tyrannical control which man feels from material goods is due to the effort he makes, whether consciously of unconsciously, to make them autonomous from their Creator.

The theology of St Symeon the New Theologian, resting on sure cosmological and anthropological premises, maintains emphatically that our natural surroundings—what we today call the environment—and creation in general cannot be excluded and isolated from man's life; indeed it plays a most essential role even in man's spiritual struggle. Characteristically he writes about the way the passion of listlessness affecting Christians engaged in the ascetic struggle is connected with "the temperature of the air" and the "depressing thickness of the south wind."[15] Undoubtedly, however, the main problem remains man's disposition and attitude towards creation and the natural environment.

This study does not presume to offer "solutions" or to present some sort of "programme" to address the terrible problems connected with land use, ecology and the environment which have piled up as a result of the irrational and unnatural use of the world which is especially characteristic of our age. But it does aim to present a dimension of the subject which is unknown to many, forgotten by others, and ignored by others again—the theological dimension, particularly as we have it from the writings and teaching of a great theologian of our Church, St Symeon the New Theologian. We attempt to look at this dimension and place it within the context not only of Scripture and the rest of the patristic tradition but also of the Church's life of liturgy and worship. The aim of this endeavor is on the one hand to present the

---

15 "Again, if I have constrained my body to excess, I make my mind clouded and sluggish, and fall once more into the same passion [of listlessness]. And there are times when the same happens to those engaged in the ascetic struggle as a result of the temperature of the air, somehow, and the depressing thickness of the south wind." *Chapters* 1.73, SC 51, p. 82.

theological dimension to the problem of relations between man and creation, and on the other to promote the eucharistic use of the world as lived out for centuries by the Orthodox Church.

The subject is treated in five chapters. Chapter One deals with God's relationship with the world, that of the Creator to His creation. It underlines the creation of the world "out of nothing" and the joint participation in this work of the three Persons of God in Trinity, as St Symeon the New Theologian himself notes when he says, "For there is One who made all things, Jesus Christ, with the Father who has no beginning and the Holy Spirit who with them is without beginning."[16] Chapter Two looks at man's position as a creature interposed between God and inanimate creation, since it was he who received the command to "till" and "keep" the world. Through the physiology of man and his creation in the image of God, we proceed to explore the place of man in the world. Chapter Three talks about the misuse of creation and the use which is contrary to nature, which is a mark of the world in its fallen state. It is noted that the Fall consists in making matter and the world autonomous, in worshipping creation "rather than the Creator," and there is discussion of ways in which the world is misused. Chapter Four presents the eucharistic use of the world, as propounded in the writings of St Symeon the New Theologian and lived by the Church. This use is diametrically contrary to the spirit of abuse of the world, consumption and impersonal individual well-being, embodying an opposite ethos and an ascetic-eucharistic mode of being and way of life. Here we also refer to the "inner principles" (*logoi*) of things in creation, which is a starting point for the theology of the eleventh-century mystical writer. Finally, Chapter Five deals with the transfiguration of the world and its restoration and renewal in Christ. It examines how the divine Incarnation and the presence of Christ in the world give created nature and the world the possibility of being

16 *Hymns* 44, SC 196, p. 104.

sanctified through the churching of the world—its grafting into the deified human Body of Christ, which is the Church—and the raising of matter to participation in life through the mystery of the Divine Eucharist.

Having read the works of St Symeon, one feels embarrassed and inadequate trying to speak or write about matters which require a knowledge and perception of the divine, when one has not experienced divine illumination. This is regarded by the holy Father as a form of idle talk, since an "idle word" is not just one which is unprofitable, but equally one which is spoken or written "before we practise it and gain knowledge of it from experience."[17] This was the greatest impediment for the author before writing this study, since he and his generation live in the consumerist, affluent society brought to us by the kingdom of money, which brings with it an immense social ferment and has many negative ramifications. For when we speak of a kingdom of money, we mean first and foremost the lack of purpose in money, the wealth which is made into an absolute, a god which incites unbridled production. This applies to the production even of religious articles, which end up becoming consumer goods, products manufactured for a certain kind of beauty. "The kingdom of money" also refers to the attitude which stems from human voracity and greed, and to the tragic way in which man is trapped by his limiteless material "needs."

If we have finally overcome our hesitations, this is due to a profound conviction regarding the promise contained in

---

17 *Ethical Discourses* I.12, SC 122 p. 306; tr. Alexander Golitzin, St Symeon the New Theologian, *On the Mystical Life*, vol. 1 (Crestwood, 1995), p. 79: "You who have not arrived yourselves at the perception and knowledge and experience of divine illumination and contemplation, how can you talk or write at all about such things without shuddering? For if we are obliged to render an account for every idle word, how much more shall we not be tried and convicted as vain babblers when our words touch on matters such as these. For vain babble is not, as some might suppose, just unedifying talk. It also applies to talk which is unsupported by practice and the knowledge won from experience."

Orthodox cosmology. This view of the universe, discovered through ascetic practice, manifests the inner, divine principle in all material things, highlights the personal dimension of the cosmos, and reveals the uniqueness of the human person. This cosmology may be able to make some cracks in the edifice of consumerism beneath which we all try, to a greater or lesser extent, to shelter, overlooking the daily violation and prostitution of the "very good" world which is a gift to us from the love of God.

I

God and the World

1. Creation of the world out of nothing

In the texts of ancient Greek literature, it is possible to identify three different ways of explaining the origin of the world. The first attempts to explain the "how" of the world, assuming its complete self-sufficiency and accepting its eternity, self-existence, and autonomy. According to this mode of interpretation, matter is eternal and preexists the work of creation, while it forms and produces beings and things. This view, which does not accept that the world has a creator, is characteristically summed up in the saying of Heraclitus, "This cosmos, the same for all, has been created by no one, whether god or man, but was always and is and shall be fire ever-living, kindled in measure and quenched in measure."[1]

The second approach—very closely related to the first—explains the genesis of the world in accordance with a primitive human attitude towards it. Again without placing the cause of the universe outside the world, it deifies the elements of physical reality themselves. This is essentially the same idea of the world as self-existent and autonomous, and also complete; in other words, properties are attributed to the world that, in contrast to the mortality and corruption of man, are characterized as divine. This belief is attributed by Plato both to ignorant barbarians and to educated Greeks: "Firstly the earth and the sun, the stars and all the universe, and the things of the seasons so well set in order, divided into years and months. And that Greeks and barbarians alike think that they are gods."[2]

1 Fragment 30; H. Diels, *Die Fragmente der Vorsokratiker* (fourth edition), I, 84.
2 *Laws* I, 886a 2-5.

The third way of explaining the world, characteristically summed up by Aristotle, refers the cause of the world to a supreme divine Principle, i.e. to some creator God;[3] whereas in Plato, God's creative work does not refer to the creation of the world out of nothing, but covers only the *ordering* of the world.[4] Very characteristic on this point is the testimony of St Athanasius the Great, who says in refutation of this position and more generally of the reasoning of Plato and his supporters, "others, Plato among them, say that god made all things out of preexisting and ungenerate matter; for god could not have made anything if matter had not already existed."[5]

So here we have three interpretations and views of the reality of the world among the ancient Greeks: 1) the world is accepted as self-existent and autonomous; 2) the elements and laws of the physical universe are made into gods; and 3) the cause of the world is traced back to some god. In these three explanations we may see in summary all the forms and variants of all later cosmological theories, which can be divided into materialistic, pantheistic and theocentric-deterministic.

In Holy Scripture, by contrast, we have a clear reminder that the whole world was made by God, and not on the basis of some preexistent matter but "out of nothing."[6] And we can discern that the theology of the Fathers of the Orthodox tradition is an organic

---

3   "Seeing the sun going round by day and the orderly movement of the other stars by night, they thought some god was the cause of such movement and good order." *On Philosophy* 2a, in *Fragmenta Selecta*, ed. W.D. Ross (Oxford 1964), p. 80. But Aristotle himself believed that matter exists and does not come into being. All that is created is the form in the particular entity, together with the movement and purpose which effect the transition from the potential to the actual. Each form, which is a shaped version of the cause of that particular entity, is called "made of a that material [*ekeininos*]." See Metaphysics IX, 1049a: "It seems that what we are talking about is not 'this thing' but 'something of that material'—just as a box is not wood, but wooden."

4   See *Timaeus* 53 b1: "when he began to order the universe," and *The Statesman* 273 D4, "god who ordered it."

5   *On the Incarnation* 2.3, PG 25.100A.

6   2 Maccabees 7:28.

development of the biblical teaching, despite the abstract modes of expression that the Fathers sometimes use.[7]

In contrast to the philosophical and even the mythical understandings, in theology creation out of nothing is presented as a consummate mystery, celebrated by God in Trinity. And this because the act of creation is not merely the shaping of a reality or the bestowal of a quality; it is the production of the very essence of created things. Creation for the Fathers means that all things emerge out of nothing by the creative energy of the word and will of God.

St Symeon the New Theologian preserves in his writings this position, fundamental to our subject. God is He who "brings the whole creation out of non-being into being by a word alone and by His own will."[8] This means that the production of creation out of nothing is not an independent or autonomous outcome. It comes from the divine word and the divine creative will and energy and not from the divine essence. Creation is not self-existent, nor is it preserved by itself; it is guarded, held together and preserved by God.

God and the world are radically distinguished. God is "uncreated, without beginning, ever existing and before all things," whereas the world "was produced and came into being." At the same time, however, they are indissolubly connected. God is "the only maker and Creator of these things." The creation, since it came into existence "out of non-being" is not able to survive on its own. But on the other hand, it does not come out of the divine essence, and in consequence, it does not coexist beside the uncreated God as an unchangeable state.[9] Thus the act of creation is not confined to the

---

7 For references to Fathers of the Church and secular writers on the subject of creation see N. Matsoukas, *The Problem of Evil; An Essay in Patristic Theology* (in Greek), Thessaloniki 1976, pp. 25-41.

8 *Hymns* 44, SC 196, p. 70.

9 *Theological Discourses* 1, SC 122, p. 108: "The Only God, the Holy Trinity, when He willed it, brought forth the heaven and earth and all that is in them out of non-being and made all the heavenly powers, and then last of all He made man; and

emergence of creation from nothingness, but is extended into a binding link which holds together and joins all existent things and the whole of creation with God.[10]

The presence of God as personal will and energy—not as essence—is immediate and active in the world. Once God creates the world out of nothing, He organizes it, adorns it, and preserves it. In order to describe God's work in creation more graphically, St Symeon the New Theologian says that God acted like some nobleman or king who constructs, organizes, and appropriately adorns the land belonging to him. He does not make the whole area one city or one extended house; instead, he divides it into several parts and then leaves one stretch of ground for arable land, designates another to be a vineyard, and leaves another fallow. He puts the dwellings in a pleasant and beautiful spot; there he builds palaces and constructs houses and baths. He puts in trees and plants in enchanting gardens, and devises every kind of recreation and delight. All this he surrounds with a fence, leaving gates that open and close to secure the area. And even though he himself is not afraid of anything, he stations guards so that the area remains closed to any ungrateful and wicked friends who might wish to present themselves, while faithful friends and grateful servants can come and go freely. This, then, was the tactic the Lord used with the first-created humans.[11]

there is nothing of the things in earth or in heaven or under the earth which was not brought forth and made out of non-being; God, the maker and creator of these things, alone is uncreated, without beginning, ever existing and existing before all..."

10 The same thought had been formulated in different words at various times by earlier Fathers too. See for example Maximus the Confessor, *Chapters on Love*, PG 90.1024B and 1025A: "In His extreme goodness, when God brought into being the rational and spiritual essence He shared four of the divine properties which bind beings together and preserve them: existence, ever-existence, goodness and wisdom." "God as being existence itself and goodness itself and wisdom itself—or to speak more truly, above all these—has altogether no opposite; but creatures, as all having existence by grace and participation..."

11 "In just this way did God act for the first man. After He had created everything out of nothing, and had made man, and had rested on the seventh day from all His works which He had made, then God planted the garden in Eden, in the East. He

God created the world as a paradise of delight in which man was to enjoy the blessedness of communion with God through partaking in and making use of God's good things. In other words the world, in the initial scheme of creation, was equivalent to paradise. The fall of man, which will be treated at greater length in a later chapter, differentiated the world from paradise. Thus in referring to the relationship between world and paradise, St Symeon stresses that in time at least, the former precedes the latter. The world could have been paradise, since it was created by God "very good," for man to enjoy. But in His omniscience God foresaw the fall of man and took account of man's persistence in his fall and lack of repentance that would lead him to self-condemnation and destruction, and so He did not leave the whole human race only in this world, which was created with Adam during the six days of creation. Offering once again the prospect of eternity, God gave man the paradise which He "planted afterwards in the East,"[12] after resting on the seventh day and ending the works of the first creation.

Having very clear ideas of cosmology and a thorough knowledge both of the biblical tradition concerning creation and of the patristic tradition prior to his own time, Symeon felt the need to clarify further the relationship between the world and paradise, clearing up misunderstandings and confused ideas on the subject. So he underlines that at the beginning of creation God did not give paradise alone to the first-formed humans, as some people think, nor did He make only paradise incorruptible. But long before paradise, He created the whole world in which we live, in other words the earth and everything in it together with the entire universe and everything that is in the universe. On the sixth day God made Adam, whom He appointed lord and king "of the whole visible creation." At that time, Eve had not yet been

planted it in a particular part of the world, made a kind of royal palace, and there He placed man whom He had made." *Ethical Discourses* I.1, SC 122, p. 180; *On the Mystical Life*, vol. 1, p. 24.

12 *Ethical Discourses* 2.3, SC 122, pp. 340–2; *On the Mystical Life*, vol. 1, p. 96.

created; nor indeed had paradise. Only this world "like a paradise" had been formed by God—a unified, incorruptible world,
but at the same time material and tangible. This was the world
God gave to Adam and his descendants to enjoy.[13]

Within the Old Testament, Symeon distinguishes three worlds.
The first is the world of the first creation with Adam and Eve. The
second world is the one saved in Noah's ark. He sees the third as
being that which begins with the calling of Abraham and goes up to
the coming of Christ and His theanthropic appearance in the world.
In one chapter of his *Ethical Discourses*, Symeon describes and examines in detail all the prefigurations, the images, and the very interesting correlations between this third world and the previous two, and
also between this and the world which came after Christ.[14]

Those of the Fathers who dealt more systematically with the
subject of creation and how the world was made have noted particularly the order, good order, and harmony prevailing in the
world. St Gregory of Nyssa says that creation is "organized with
order and orderliness and consistency."[15] This order and
well-ordered state also provide an interpretation of the fact that
God planted paradise after the end of the seventh day of creation—thus inaugurating the eighth day. The seven days form a
prefiguration of the "seven ages," i.e. of the time extending from
the end of creation to the second coming of Christ. This explains
why God "planted paradise after these things": it is precisely
because the eighth day symbolizes the life of the age to come, and

13 *Ethical Discourses* 1.1, SC 122, p. 174; *On the Mystical Life*, vol. 1, p. 21. Cf.
    Anastasius of Sinai, PG 89.540-41 and 961-70.

14 He entitles this chapter: "That the first world brought into being in the beginning
    was followed by two other worlds, the last of which is a type of the things to take
    place after this, being a mean between those of old and those to come later. And of
    what the Promised Land was an image, and so forth." 2.5, SC 122, pp. 354-358;
    Ethical Discourses 1, pp. 101-104.

15 "For the concord and sympathy of all things with each other, organized with order
    and orderliness and consistency, is the first, archetypal and true music." *On the
    Inscriptions of the Psalms* 3, PG 44.441C.

paradise is the sign of that life. And He did not number the eighth day within the cycle of seven days, because these days come round and repeat themselves every week, whereas the eighth day had to remain apart from them "as having neither beginning nor end."[16]

The order, beauty, and good order of creation, the sympathy and concord among God's creations, form the music for the festival of the universe to His glory. The foundation on which the world is built and established is the glory of God. This is what vivifies the world, and it is this that the world tells of ceaselessly: "The heavens are telling the glory of God, and the firmament proclaims His handiwork."[17] Moreover, the very existence of the world is an eternal doxology to God. The existence of the world, the universe which "God saw that it was good,"[18] is a "mystical harmony... forming a hymn to the power which controls the universe."[19] And as it has very aptly been remarked, "in this symphony of heavenly music, this chorus in which all creation takes part, the Creator is composer and director."[20]

Symeon gives expression to this doxological dimension of the existence of the world in one of his hymns, together with his personal wonder at the wisdom of God to which creation testifies. He calls us to wonder at the abyss of God's wisdom, observing the whole creation: the sky, the sun, the stars, "mother earth," the "earthly world," all the varieties of animals and birds with their different forms and calls, and again the sea with all its breadth and

---

16   *Ethical Discourses* 1.1, SC 122, pp. 180-2. See also Basil the Great, *On the Holy Spirit* 27, 66, PG 32.189Bf. and Gregory of Nyssa, *On the Inscriptions of the Psalms* 2.5, PG 44.504. See also G. Mantzaridis, *Sociology of Christianity* (in Greek) (Thessaloniki, 1985), 109.

17   Ps 18:2; all Psalm references are given according to the Septuagint numbering. Translations follow the Revised Standard Version, modified where necessary to reflect the Septuagint text.

18   Gen 1:18.

19   Gregory of Nyssa, *On the Inscriptions of the Psalms* 3, PG 44.441BC.

20   Hieromonk Gregorios, "The World as Liturgical Place" (in Greek), Synaxi 14 (Athens, 1985), 22.

vastness and the bounds that define it. All this certainly does not amount to "nature worship," but to ways of leading us up to the incomprehensible wisdom and knowledge of God through the greatness and beauty of created things.[21]

From the "study" of God's "incomprehensible wisdom," we learn the great truth that God does not despise any of His creations. He honors even the smallest component and makes it participate in the mystery of creation. In this way, the dynamism with which God endowed the world from the beginning is activated and put to use, and nature's proper mode of functioning is manifested. The difference between man's creations and God's lies precisely in the fact that God creates *out of nothing*. Hence His creations have real existence and real dynamism because, being created out of nothing, they are not grounded in themselves. Their "self," their nature on its own is changeable and corruptible, threatened constantly by ontological annihilation, by the non-being out of which created things came; so they are grounded instead in the all-powerful will of God, absolutely constant and full of love and beyond any notion of beginning or end, change, or alteration. God's creations are real and open to eternity in a divine manner (beyond anything that man can understand) because they exist thanks to the eternal and unchangeable will of God.[22]

2. *The world as a work of God in Trinity*

God is love (1 Jn 4:16). Love is the substructure of life itself (uncreated and created) and the organic expression of it as a basic

---

21 "O the depth of riches and divine knowledge,
   O the depth of Your wisdom, my God all-bountiful!
   That from the greatness and beauty of created things
   you might learn of the incomprehensible Wisdom of God
   and of the spiritual combat,
   which the Maker of all has depicted in advance..."

22 See D. Staniloae, "The World as Gift and Sacrament of God's Love," *Sobornost* 5.9 (1969), 671f., and P. Nellas, "Christians in the World" (in Greek), *Synaxi* 13 (1985), 8f.

element in creation. The creation of all things out of nothing and the relationship between God and the world would be incomprehensible if there did not exist the divine love which is, in the final analysis, God's mode of being. While for God, love is a mode of being, it is offered to created beings and developed in them as a gift of the three Persons of the Holy Trinity. The world was created and is preserved and saved by the love of God in Trinity.

In the Orthodox tradition there are many writings in which the trinitarian character of the creation of the world, and more generally of divine revelation, is clearly evident. Characteristic is the prayer for the blessing of water in the service of Baptism. This refers to the creation and blessing of the world with the interpenetration of the three Persons of God in Trinity: "For Thou by Thy will bringest all things from nonexistence into being, by Thy might Thou dost hold together the creation, by Thy providence Thou governest the world... For Thou being God uncircumscribed, without beginning and beyond speech didst come upon earth taking the form of a servant, becoming in the likeness of men... Therefore, O King who lovest mankind, do Thou Thyself be present also now by the descent of Thy Holy Spirit and sanctify this water...." More generally, in all her prayers our Church tries to lead the believer up from the nature around us to the Creator, from the created to the uncreated Holy Trinity. All the services begin with the confession and doxology of the one God ("Blessed is our God...") and end with a doxological reference to the Trinitarian Unity (of the Father and of the Son and of the Holy Spirit). As the precondition for the world there is the trinitarian God, who created all things, and governs, preserves and holds them together, the Lord of all life and "of every visible and invisible creation."[23]

---

23 See further Protopresbyter Georgios Metallinos, "Ecological Correspondences and Discrepancies between Hellenism and Christianity—Their Attitude to the Environment" (in Greek), *Koinonia* (Athens, 1985), vol. 4, 501.

A commonplace in the patristic tradition is the belief that the trinitarian God is in some way imaged in the whole of creation and that the unseen things of God are understood through creation, since creation is an icon of God Himself. Of course, impersonal nature images the trinitarian God without being able to progress to a likeness to God by grace and a consummation, because it lacks the receptivity of rational beings. Nevertheless, the whole articulation and structure of creation is an image of God in Trinity, and for this reason it comes alive and finds its worth only in relationship with Him and dependence on Him. The beauty of created things is not the one-dimensional principle of efficient cause, but the manifestation of the mode of divine operation, or energy, at once unified and trinitarian, which reflects the mystery of the unified and also trinitarian mode of divine life. The existence of creation is a trinitarian hymnody and a manifestation of God in Trinity: "One God and Father of us all, who is above all and through all and in all," as St Paul says.[24] Thus it becomes comprehensible why God, the cause of creation, is hymned by His creation in a trinitarian manner.[25]

Thus St Symeon exhorts every human being not only to be led by existent things to the belief that there is a God who is the cause of creation, but also to learn and understand the way in which He

24 Eph 4:6.
25 A passage which has by now become a classic in theology is the following from Maximus the Confessor's *To Thalassius, On Various Difficulties* 13, PG 90.296B:
    "For it is on the basis of existent things that we believe in the existence of God, the one who can properly be said to exist. Thus too from the essential difference in form among existent things we are taught of the existence of His Wisdom which is innate according to essence, and which holds existent things together. And again, from the movement essential to each form of being we learn of the existence of His life which is innate according to essence, which brings existent things to fulfilment. We learn this from a wise contemplation of creation, receiving information about the Holy Trinity, the Father the Son and the Holy Spirit. For the Word is eternal power of God, being consubstantial, and the Holy Spirit is eternal divinity.
    "They stand condemned, therefore, who have not learnt from contemplation of existent things the cause of those things and the properties belonging to that cause by nature, namely power and divinity."

exists. From the difference that exists between existent things one learns of the force which binds them together, God the Word, the personified wisdom of God, and of the Holy Spirit who is the life-giving force in existent things. From the apophatic approach to the universe one learns the apophatic knowledge and understanding of God.[26] If man is able to know the height of heaven or demonstrate the course of the sun, moon and stars and what they are made of, to know the bounds and size of the earth, if he can even count the sands of the sea and above all can investigate his own nature, only then will he be able to interpret the work of God's wisdom and understand his Creator:

> How in Trinity, the Oneness without confusion
> and in Oneness, Trinity without division.[27]

At this point, the dependence of creation on the Creator is established in such a way that creation cannot exist or move or progress or come to perfection on its own. From this form of dependency we understand that the radical distinction that exists between God and creation comes from the fact that creation has no likeness to the divine essence. As something created by God, however, it attains to a relative likeness which comes about by grace according to the divine energy.[28]

In the thought of St Symeon the New Theologian, the Holy Trinity exists as the center and connecting bond of the whole world,[29] since the world came into being "out of non-being" solely by the word and will of the trinitarian God:

> Glory, praise, hymns, thanksgiving,
> to Him who brought the whole creation

26 "For if the creature were to learn all about the Creator and what He is like, and understand Him totally, and were able to express it in words and write it down—then the words would be greater than the creator." *Hymns* 21, SC 174, p. 140.

27 *Ibid.*

28 See N. Matsoukas, *World, Man and Communion according to Maximus the Confessor* (in Greek) (Athens, 1980), p. 59.

29 *Chapters* 3.2, SC 51, p. 120.

> out of nothing into being
> by His word alone and by His own will,
> the God of all, in Trinity
> of persons, in one essence worshipped![30]

All three Persons of the Godhead take part in this creation:

> For there is one who made all things
> Jesus Christ, with the Father who has no beginning
> and the Holy Spirit also without beginning.[31]

It is nonetheless true, of course, that the manner in which vestiges of the Trinity are to be found in created things and in the world cannot be expressed except in relative images and conventional concepts. For as St Maximus the Confessor says, "the Divinity... remains inconceivable even when thought of, and ineffable even when spoken of."[32] Nevertheless, the Father "intends," the Word "activates," and the Holy Spirit "perfects" created things.[33] Creation is the common work of the Holy Trinity. But the three Persons are the cause of created things in a way that is different, but at the same time unified. The Trinitarian One "brings out of non-being," "gives being," and "ineffably holds in existence" heaven and earth, the sun, moon and stars, all four-footed beasts, and reptiles and wild animals, "birds of every kind" and "all sea creatures."[34] His command protects and preserves all things.[35] The Wisdom of the Father exercises providence for all things; "before all ages" He intends the created things of the world, wills them, and loves them. Furthermore, the true beauty of the world reveals this providence and will and love of the Father. This revelation is *logos*, a meaning, a "word." It is the

---

30 *Hymns* 44, SC 196.70.
31 *Hymns* 44, SC 196.104.
32 *Letter* 6, PG 91.432C.
33 See Basil the Great, *On the Holy Spirit* 16, 38, PG 32.136AB and Gregory of Nazianzus, Hom. 45.5, PG 36.629A.
34 *Hymns* 45, SC 196.106.
35 *Ibid.*

manifestation of the energy of the Son and Word, "through whom all things were made." And this "One," which "brings down" and "creates" and "brings all things into being by a word," "holds all these things together by the Spirit of power," i.e. with the life-giving power of the Holy Spirit.[36]

This theology of St Symeon's concerning the relation of the Son and Word of God to creation coincides exactly with that of St John the Theologian as it is formulated at the beginning of his Gospel: "All things were made through Him, and without Him was not anything made that was made" (Jn 1:3).[37] The Father, the Mind, bears the "personified Word" who "extends through the whole world,"[38] while the Holy Spirit is to be found in the order and well-ordered state of the world indicated, as we have seen already, in the fact that "he did not attach to the previous seven" days of creation the eighth day, on which God planted paradise in the east.[39]

Finally, the term "creation" also contains a sense of the care of the Creator, who creates through the Word out of love, for the enjoyment and happiness of every creature. Then all things find their fullness, their basis, their true substance and existence through personal relationship with God in creation itself, since the creative Word by His Incarnation partakes in the creation in a way that is supranatural, but at the same time material and historical. This is why the verb "to create" (*ktizo*) is used in Scripture in this sense: "In Him [i.e. Christ as the Word, the principle of creation] all things were created."[40] The Word of God reveals the

---

36 *Ibid.*, 104. Cf Maximus the Confessor, *Theological Chapters*, PG 90.1209A: "The Holy Spirit is in all things in a manner which is simple, inasmuch as He is that which holds all things together and exercises providence for them, and sets in motion the seminal potentialities in their nature."

37 *Hymns* 21, SC 174.148.

38 *Ibid.*, 134.

39 *Ethical Discourses* 1.1, SC 122.182; see above, p. 19.

40 Col 1:16.

Father to the world, He pours out the Holy Spirit abundantly upon creation, and He shows humans and the rest of creation that He is the "creator and maker of all things."[41]

3. The relationship between creation and its Maker

The biblical understanding of creation and its relationship with God shows itself in one of the key words in the Hebrew language, the verb *bara,* "to create." This word in Scripture is used exclusively to express the creative power and will and energy of God. It signifies creation out of nothing. For this reason, it is never used of human constructions and creations. At the same time, it indicates that God is not only Creator, but also sustainer, governor, and ruler of the world. This is why He intervenes in its history. Parallel with this, another poetic text of the Old Testament, Psalm 103—the opening psalm of Vespers—testifies to this relationship between the world and the Maker when it sings of the cosmic liturgy—the way the world functions—by way of a hymn to God. There the world is recognized not only as His work, but as a supreme example of His creation that was "very good." Again, in another psalm (Psalm 18) the world is described as the bridal chamber in which the Word of God weds man: "In the sun has He set His tent, and He comes forth like a bridegroom leaving his chamber, and like a giant He runs his course with joy."[42]

Many other liturgical texts also refer to the dependence of creation on the Creator and the relationship of beings with their maker.[43] In the writings of the Church Fathers, too, it is stressed

41 *Hymns* 53, SC 196.232-4.

42 Ps 18:6. See further the study of Hieromonk Gregorios, "The World as Liturgical Place" (in Greek), *Synaxi* 14 (Athens, 1985), 22f.

43 The anaphora prayer in the Liturgy of St James the Brother of the Lord begins as follows: "It is truly right and fitting, proper and our bounden duty to praise Thee, to bless Thee, to worship Thee, to glorify Thee, to give thanks to Thee, the Maker of all creation visible and invisible, the Treasure of eternal good things, the Fount of life and of immortality, the God and Master of all; who art hymned by the heavens and the heavens of heavens and all their powers, the sun and moon and all the choir

that the whole of creation is a place of God's presence, and creation itself proclaims its relationship with and dependence on God the only Creator.[44] But while the Fathers refer to the relationship between God and the world, they emphasize at the same time that this relationship presupposes otherness and radical difference. Besides, this follows from the truth of the creation of the world out of nothing. St Symeon the New Theologian stresses that God, having an essence and nature that is uncircumscribed, is both within the world and outside it. Attempting to reply to the question, "How are You outside created things, how are You also within them, and how neither inside nor outside?" he says that all created things are within God "since He holds together all things," and at the same time outside God because created beings are separated from the uncreated God.

> All things I bear within Me
> since I hold together all creation;
> but I am outside all things
> being separated from everything.[45]

The existence of God as Cause of all, Creator and Maker of created things, explains how He is at the same time separate from the things he has made.[46] The human mind is unable to comprehend how God, who "holds together all things," is able to be

of stars, earth, sea and all that is in them." The same relationship is underlined by the prayer of the Blessing of Waters at Theophany, which is repeated in the rite of Baptism and is the work of Sophronius, Patriarch of Jerusalem: "The sun sings Thy praises; the moon glorifies Thee; the stars supplicate before Thee; the light obeys Thee; the deeps are afraid at Thy presence... at Thine Epiphany the whole creation sang Thy praises." *The Festal Menaion*, tr. Mother Mary and Archimandrite Kallistos Ware (London, 1969), p. 356.

44 St Cyril of Jerusalem writes in this regard: "Day to day pours forth speech, and night to night declares knowledge. They virtually cry out to the heretics who have not ears, saying through their good order that there is no other God but the Creator who has set bounds for all things and arranged them in order;" *Catecheses* 9.6, PG 33.645A. Cf. Ps 18.2.

45 *Hymns* 23, SC 174.190; cf. also *Hymns* 29, SC 174.322-4.

46 "For the Creator—how will he not be outside all His creations?" (*ibid.*)

outside all created things, and also to "fill" all things while
remaining at the same time "wholly outside, ineffably."[47] But the
essence of created things, while being a result of the divine creative energy, has no similarity to the divine essence. This distinction between the divine essence, which is uncreated, and the
essence of created things which is created, gives us the possibility
of speaking of God as existing simultaneously within the world
and also outside the world: "for [God] is uncreated and outside all
created things, uncreated in the midst of the created."[48] Again,
God is and exists as love; and love is an "all-creating light" that
illumines all created things and all the world, without coming
from the world or having anything in common with any created
thing in this world.[49]

The possibility that man has of perceiving the presence of God
through the created world is something that Symeon stresses in
many of his writings.[50] Yet this possibility is characterized by a
certain apophatic quality. The apophatic quality of God's presence in the world relates also to the way in which man is to
approach Him. For those who try to see God with bodily eyes, He
is nowhere to be found, since He is invisible. But for those who
are able to perceive with spiritual senses, He is everywhere,
because He is present. Being within the universe and outside the
universe, He is at once near to those who desire to feel His presence and far from those who deny it.[51]

Since, then, the trinitarian God is imaged in nature, it is
through the relation between the trinitarian God and the world

47 *Hymns* 42, SC 196.42-4.
48 *Hymns* 17, SC 174.30.
49 *Ibid.*
50 See *Catecheses* 2, SC 96.248; cf. Ps 138:8-10.
51 *Chapters* 1.1, SC 51.40: "To those who look with bodily eyes God is nowhere, for
    He in invisible; but for those who perceive spiritually He is everywhere, for He is
    present. For He is within everything and outside everything, hence also His salva-
    tion is near to those who fear Him and far from sinners."

that we can clarify the relationship between natural and supranatural revelation, a relationship completely interwoven with the work of creation. The "He is nowhere, for He in invisible" and the "He is everywhere, for He is present" of God show the mistake of making natural revelation autonomous and the error of looking at it without reference to supranatural revelation with which it is indissolubly and organically connected. Anyone who is able to hear the hymn of creation to God in Trinity is not only properly placed as regards natural revelation but has also made progress through the spiritual stages of perfection. Natural revelation is the receptivity of rational beings in itself, while supranatural revelation is the truth which saves and deifies.[52]

Again, a summary look at how the *name* functions in the different religious traditions is indicative enough of the significance that it carries, which goes far beyond the conventional interpretation of names as mere signs serving only to replace objects. It is known that when someone bears a name, that means that he is received into communion and relationship, while giving something a name indicates that one brings it into a realm of communion and relationship. Naming gives the possibility of referring, calling and invoking.[53] In the Jewish tradition, knowing a name indicates a form of dominance over what is named. When Adam gave names to the beasts of the earth,[54] he manifested his dominance in creation, his kingly rank. Having children is seen as a blessing because the children will keep alive the father's name.[55] This significance of the name makes the name of God inaccessible

52   See N. Matsoukas, *op. cit.*, 56, where more is said about how the relation between natural and supernatural revelation is regarded both in Orthodox theology and in the West.

53   For Plato, naming cannot be done arbitrarily but can only be the product of intention: "Not everyone is a creator of names, but only one who looks to the name belonging by nature to each thing and is able to embody its form in letters and syllables," *Cratylus*, 390e 1-4.

54   Gen 2:19-20.

55   See Gen 48:16.

to the Israelites. Both Jacob in his struggle with God[56] and Moses before the Burning Bush[57] ask to know God's name, which is only assurance of the theophany. In the New Testament Christ gives an assurance that He has come in His Father's name.[58] The revelation of God consists in the manifestation of His Name—"I have manifested Thy Name to men"[59]—and the Disciples do mighty works in the name of Christ.[60] This biblical understanding of the name lies at the root of the entire eastern Orthodox Tradition, and especially of the hesychast tradition.[61]

St Symeon the New Theologian talks about the name of God and the name of God's creations, thus adding another valuable dimension to the subject of the relation between creation and Maker. The Son and Word of God, he says, "extends through the whole world"[62] and manifests to it both Himself and His Father, pouring out in abundance His All-Holy Spirit and revealing His Name to men, while by His works He shows that He is the creator and maker of all."[63] Nevertheless, there is no name which can be attributed to God and can define God, since all names and objects and words came into being at God's creative command. He gave names to created things and gave each thing the possibility of being named in a special way, just as He gave certain created things the capacity to give names to others as a sign of their dominance over them. While the creature names other creatures or is called by a name, the name of the Maker still remains unknown

56 Gen 32:22-32.
57 Ex 3:13.
58 Jn 5:43.
59 Jn 17:6.
60 Cf. Mk 9:38-39.
61 St John of the Ladder, talking about the method of mental prayer, says that the "art" lies in the repetition of the Name of Jesus: "Scourge enemies with the Name of Jesus; for in heaven or on earth there is no more powerful weapon." *The Ladder* 20.6.
62 *Hymns* 21, SC 174.134
63 *Hymns* 53, SC 196.232-4.

to men, to whom He is known as "He who is, God inexpressible" as He has revealed Himself.[64]

So on this point too Symeon identifies himself totally with the theological tradition of the Orthodox Christian East, where "to call" and "to give names" denotes a personal activity or "energy" and the realization of a personal relationship, while the things named are given their names on the basis of the difference in personal energy which they embody.[65] Again, as the thing named is not identified in essence with the name-giver, or even with the energy of the name-giver, so also the word or the will of God is not identified with the creatures themselves—just as the will of an artist is not identified with the work of art itself, i.e. with the result of his personal creative energy. Hence St John of Damascus writes, "I venerate [matter] not as God, but as being filled with divine energy and grace."[66] The thing made is different both in essence and in energy from its maker: "The energy is something else that the 'energizer' is not. For God 'energizes' and makes created things, but He Himself is uncreated," as St Gregory Palamas stresses;[67] while according to the expression favored by St Basil, "artistic skill in the work of art" is something different from "artistic skill in the artist."[68]

64 *Hymns* 21, SC 174.150:
  "What would you call the Creator of all?
  For names and things and words
  all came into being at God's command.
  For he gave names to His works,
  to His works gave power to give names in turn.
  His works call each other and are called by different names,
  but His name never has been known to us
  other than, He who is, God inexpressible, as Scripture has said."
65 See Basil, *Against Eunomius* 1.7, PG 29.525A.
66 *Second Apology* 14, PG 94.1300B; Basil, *Against Eunomius 2.32*, PG 29.648A: "The works that are made are indicative of power and wisdom and art, but not of the essence itself; and nor do they necessarily represent the power of the Maker in its fullness." See also V. Lossky, *The Mystical Theology of the Eastern Church* (London, 1957), pp. 93ff.
67 *Natural and Theological Chapters*, PG 150.1220C.
68 *On the Holy Spirit* 26(61), PG 32.180.

The Church Fathers define the world as a *place* of God, since it forms the sphere in which the manifestation of His personal energy becomes apparent: "It is called a 'place of God' where His energy becomes manifest," as St John of Damascus says quite specifically.[69] St Symeon the New Theologian underlines that the realm of earthly reality is a place of God because He who made it is known from His creations. The beauty of created things draws man towards God their creator, and moves him to a doxological relationship with "the Maker of all."[70] In order, however, for the world to be revealed to man as a dimensionless *place* of the divine personal energy, it is necessary for man to remain "within his own limits." Only thus is he able to achieve the state of going outside himself and transcending his own individuality that makes possible the experiential approach to the personal existence of God. In the context of man's personal relationship with the "Maker of all"—a relationship whose hallmark is faith—the world ceases to be given a conventional autonomy as a neutralized object valued only for its usefulness: the world now "gives space" for God's relationship with man.[71] The human being who has the mind of Christ and wants to know the external beauty of created things discovers that God is accessible within the reality of the created world. This does not, however, remove God's natural distance from the world, which is the distance of the uncreated nature from the created.

Thus man is able "from created things correspondingly to wonder at their Creator," but he cannot confuse uncreated and created natures or identify creation with the Creator and worship created things, ignoring their Maker.[72] On the contrary, from the grandeur and beauty of created things man is able to sense and

---

69 *On the Orthodox Faith* 1.13, PG 94.852A.
70 *Theological Discourses* 2, SC 122.146.
71 *Ibid.*
72 *Ethical Discourses* 6, SC 129, p. 138. See also Rom 1:25.

know the Maker better, and his intellect can be led up "to contemplation of Him" while the longing "to understand the Maker"
is kindled in his soul.[73] Then he realizes that his closeness to God
in the world is not by nature but by place; in other words, it is a
closeness created by his personal relationship to God, because "all
things are set apart from God, not by place but by nature."[74] He
understands that it is not the world that "contains," "gives space"
to God; it is the will and energy of God that "gives space" to the
world, a space "outside" God which is at the same time a *place* of
God.[75]

God unoriginate and uncreated is not only the Creator of
"both visible and intelligible" creation, but also the Lord and
Master "who alone holds authority" over it.[76] So when in Scripture the devil is called "prince of this world"[77] he is not understood as being the ruler and master of the world, since "he does
not have authority even over swine."[78] He is referred to as ruler of
the world because he dominates and rules those who attach themselves to him by their desire for money and for all those other
things that he makes use of to separate humans from God.[79] And
it is very characteristic that the words *symvolon* ("symbol") and
diavolos ("devil," literally "slanderer") have a common root in the
Greek verb *vallo*, in its sense of "to place." But while the devil *sep-
arates* (*dia-vallo* ="put apart"), the symbol *unites* (*syn-vallo* ="put
together"). This is why the Church in her worship and sacramental life uses symbols as "loci" testifying that the thing symbolized
is truly present, while trying to keep her believers away from the

73 *Ibid.*
74 John of Damascus, *On the Orthodox Faith* 1.13, PG 94.853D.
75 *Hymns* 23, SC 174.190. See also Theophilus of Antioch, *To Autolycus* 2.3, PG
     6.1049D: "God... is not contained, but He Himself is the place of all things."
76 *Hymns* 24, SC 174.240. See also *Hymns 37, ibid.*, p. 458.
77 Jn 14:30.
78 Cf. Mt 8:30ff.
79 *Ethical Discourses* 11, SC 129.370-2; *On the Mystical Life*, vol. 2, p. 148.

influence and domination of the devil.[80] The devil is also called
the prince of darkness, because through his pride he fell away
from the realm of light where he was originally and became an
heir of darkness for ever. God, by contrast, has not bequeathed
His authority over the world to anyone, but "rules with authority
by nature over everything"[81] as Creator and Maker of all creation.

God has authority over creation: He "rules with authority by
nature over everything." But this does not mean that God's relationship with creation is that of a despot to his slaves. St Symeon
the New Theologian particularly stresses the difference between
God's relationship with man and creation and the relationship
between powerful men in the world and those who are weak.
Almost all humans, he says, shun the poor and weak; earthly
kings cannot bear even to set eyes on them, noblemen loathe
them, while the rich look down their noses at them and, if they
happen to meet them, go right past them as if they did not exist.
God, however, never ceases to be father and friend and brother
to these "rejects" among his creatures. Furthermore, "He willed
even to become incarnate, in order to become like us in all
things except sin, and make us sharers in His glory and His
Kingdom."[82] God's relationship with the world is and remains a
relationship of service, humility, and self-emptying, not one of
power and force.

4. The dialectic of created and uncreated

According to the teaching of the Cappadocian Fathers on creation, when God "took it into His mind and began to bring into
being things that were not, at the same time He conceived what
the world should be like, and produced with it the matter

---

80 "Drive far from him every evil and unclean spirit that lies hidden and makes its lair
   in his heart;" Prayer for making a catechumen.
81 *Ethical Discourses* 11, SC 129.370-2; *On the Mystical Life*, vol. 2, p. 148.
82 *Catechetical Orations* 2, SC 96.250.

appropriate for its form."[83] God's "conceiving," of course, refers
to the form, but this can never be distinguished from the matter,
i.e. from the concrete realization of that form as an entity, since,
as St Gregory the Theologian says, "God conceives... and the conception was a work, fulfilled by the Word and perfected by the
Spirit."[84] So there is no difference between God's will and His
energy, which is the process of actualizing and giving substance to
His word. The word of God is realized immediately "in the substance and form of a creation,"[85] and the work of God means a
word: "for with God, the work is a word."[86]

The whole world, sensible and intelligible, is the creation of
the one and only God. There is no possibility of another God by
nature "equal in power," or "of the same nature" with the creator
emerging or coming into being, just as it is not possible for the
creature to become consubstantial with the Maker.[87] The distinction between created and uncreated and the corresponding preeminence of the uncreated over the created is a given in
St Symeon's theology:

> For how could the created
> ever become equal to the uncreated?
> For in comparison with Him
> who ever is the same, without beginning, uncreated,
> all created things are inferior.[88]

Creation does not originate from the uncreated divine essence,
but from the uncreated divine will which from eternity holds the
principles of beings. This radical distinction between the essence of

83 Basil, *Hexaemeron* II.2, PG 29.33A.
84 Hom. 45 (*Second Homily on the Pascha*), 5, PG 36.629A. See also John of Damascus, *On the Orthodox Faith*, PG 94.865A: "God creates by conceiving, and the conception constitutes a work."
85 Basil, *Against Eunomius*, PG 29.736C.
86 Gregory of Nyssa, *Hexaemeron*, PG 44.73A.
87 *Hymns* 35, SC 174.446.
88 *Ibid.*

God and that of creatures rules out any likeness between God and creation—even rational creation—according to essence, without, of course, thereby ruling out man's deification and likeness to God by grace. The fact that created things cannot be equated with the Creator, and their "inferiority" in relation to Him, is explained by their createdness and their dependence on God their Maker.

When man tries to explain the miraculous, the clash between divine energy and the laws of nature, and searches to find an answer, he is equating God with the force of the laws of nature, which ultimately means falling into idolatry. In consequence, any such attempt either ignores or overlooks the preeminence of the uncreated over the created, as this is expressed by St Symeon and Orthodox theology. This theology never isolates a miracle as a divine appearance which is bound to conflict with the laws of nature, which must either abolish them, or suspend them, or keep them intact in any number of ways. The miracle is God's relationship with the world in itself, as it necessarily follows from the mystery of creation out of nothing, realized in creation's dependence on God and its differentiation from Him. God acts in the created world in an uncreated manner and in consequence never comes into conflict with the natural, physical structure of creation, since the divine energy does not have a physical and created quality. The events and phenomena of the world may be determined by all sorts of laws and have all kinds of interdependence between them. But no relationship that God has with the world suspends or abolishes these laws. The divine energy which acts in the reality of this world and furthers the mystery of the divine economy cannot come into conflict with human powers or weaknesses as some human "energy" might. We can even see the will of God in every event of history, but we can never identify or equate the divine energies with the limits of an objective event or an action of any kind.[89]

89 N. Matsoukas, *op. cit.*, p. 66. On the relationship between history and the mystery

Man, like the whole of the world, is made up of two components: the material and the spiritual, the visible and the invisible,
the sensible and the intelligible. "Man being twofold, made up of
soul and body, the world also was made like him, visible and
invisible..."[90] These two elements of man and the world, the
material and the spiritual, the visible and the invisible, coexist and
are in a certain way coinherent. Both of them, while being created, have a corresponding receptivity in their relationship with
the uncreated God. Rational beings have the capacity to see the
immaterial and uncreated light even with the physical element in
their being.

> Having cleansed once more the immaterial mind which was
> immersed in the desire
> of material passions, and the taste of pleasures,
> we see the immaterial light in material things in an immaterial way;
> we see the light which, as I have said, was God, in manner supremely
> unoriginate,
> invisible to sensible and material eyes,
> unapproachable to the spiritual eyes of the heart.[91]

The immaterial nature of the mind is a distinguishing feature
in relation to the material body, but it is bodily and material relative to the uncreated and bodiless God. The same applies to man's
soul, which is totally immaterial and supplies the spiritual eye of
the mind. While it is "held ineffably" between corruptible and
incorruptible, it is able to see "intelligible and immaterial things
in an immaterial way."[92]

The human mind is incapable of conceiving of God, who is
"above everything." It is unable to encompass Him or to extend so
as to manage to see Him who holds together all things and is

of the divine economy see the interesting views of Vasileios P. Stoyannos, *The Resurrection of the Dead* (in Greek) (Thessaloniki, 1977), pp. 57-67.

90 *Chapters* 3.62, SC 51bis, p. 158.
91 *Hymns* 38, SC 174.474.
92 *Ibid.*

outside everything, even though He fills all things with His presence.[93] All things are within God, while God is within and outside all things. At the same time, however, the created is totally distinct from the uncreated. The sky, although it is visibly stretched out, does not impede the rays of immaterial light from coming into the world. Being material, it is outside immaterial things—not, of course, in spatial terms, but as to its nature and essence. For the immaterial God is separate from material things, without having a particular place outside them, since God is neither bounded by anything nor circumscribed. By His word and uncreated energy God "brings forth all things in Himself." By His very nature, He is totally separate from created things and, while bearing all things within Himself, is at the same time outside everything.[94]

The origin and derivation of creation from the One God in Trinity ensures unity and cohesion among all beings, even though they are divided into material and immaterial, sensible and intelligible, visible and invisible. The common origin of beings, together with the createdness that distinguishes them, forms the bond of cohesion of the entire creation, which is held together by God Himself,[95] who, while being everywhere, remains "separate from all things material and created which were brought into being by Him."[96] But the unity, coherence and common origin of creation testifies to the unified and dynamic character in the relation between cosmology and anthropology. The one world cannot be examined without reference to the other, nor can either

93 "Him who is beyond everything, what mind could comprehend,
    or could encompass, or could extend entire
    so as to see entire Him who holds all together,
    who is outside all, filling everything and the whole universe,
    and who Himself again is wholly outside all, ineffably?"
    Hymns 42, SC 196, pp. 42-4.
94 *Hymns* 38, SC 174.470.
95 See *Hymns* 42, SC 196.42.
96 *Hymns* 38, SC 174.470.

one of the two elements of creation be looked at in isolation and independently from its relationship with the other. Enquiry into man and the world in Orthodox theology knows nothing of the watertight divisions and absolutes accepted at times by philosophy, because the relationship that exists between man and the world, and the more general structuring of creation by the Creator, make it quite impossible to have any view of rational creation without referring to and coming through everything else that makes up the sensible world in which man lives.

While man in his state of sin and fallenness expresses the split between the sensible and intelligible worlds, deified man bears witness to the unity and cohesion of the two worlds, since his life participates perfectly well in both. St Symeon the New Theologian uses a characteristic text of another Father "famed in theology," St Gregory the Theologian, in order to underline that deified man is "a mingled worshipper, earthly and heavenly, transient and immortal, king over things on earth but subject to the king above, a perfect initiate of the visible creation and an initiate also of the intelligible."[97]

---

97 *Catechetical Orations* 28, SC 113.160. See also Gregory of Nazianzus, Hom. 38, *On the Theophany*, 11, PG 36.324A.

2

THE WORLD AND MAN

1. The physiology of man

In Orthodox theology, man stands as a mirror and also a summation of the world: it is in him that the entire creation is "given shape." The truth about man becomes the measure of truth about the world, since man is regarded as "microcosm" (world on a small scale) and the world as "macroanthropos" (man on a large scale). Man is a "microcosm" which images the entire world. He is an entire world, which contains—not just symbolically, but actually—all the physical, chemical, and spiritual components of the world. The classic expression of the correspondence between the world and man is that of St Maximus the Confessor: "He maintained that the whole world, comprising visible and invisible, is a man; and again that man, composed of soul and body, is a world..." Man and the world coexist in an indissoluble relationship and unity. Hence the interchange of terms, where the world is called a man and man a world. In the world we have the natural otherness of sensible and intelligible, with the intelligible element as the unifying force. In man, the natural otherness is body and soul, where the soul unifies the organic synthesis of these two elements (body and soul). Hence man and the created world are linked together by their very creation and nature in a firm and indissoluble relationship and form one organic unity and whole, the sensible and intelligible universe.[1]

1 *Mystagogy* 7, PG 91.684D-685A. For man as microcosm and the world as "macroanthropos," see Lars Thunberg's study *Microcosm and Mediator* (Lund, 1965), pp. 140-152. See also Hans Urs von Balthasar, *Kosmische Liturgie* (Einsiedeln, 1961), pp. 169-175.

According to Scripture, and more particularly what is said in Genesis (chapters 1-3), man is a bipartite being, at once biological and spiritual. God formed man from the dust of the earth, and, breathing upon his face, transmitted the spirit to him, so that he would become a living material-spiritual being.[2] The material and "earthy" aspect of man is stressed in the New Testament too. Man is "from the earth," a "man of dust."[3] One of his basic structural elements is the soil, in other words his physical and biological components. From this point of view, he is a part of the physical creation and a biological being, which in its structure and function is not much different from any other physical beings. His material qualities may take a higher form than those of plants and animals (as seen for instance in his power of speech); but materiality is still a fundamental and inalienable component of his being, so that it is impossible to conceive of man apart from his physical and biological existence. According to the theological view of things, then, all the levels of existence belonging to the various forms in the created world are to be found in man. This is why the physiology of man has a direct relationship to Orthodox cosmology, and is of fundamental concern to it.

St Symeon the New Theologian, understanding this relationship and underlining the particular interest of the study of man in relation to the rest of creation that surrounds him, often speaks of the physiology of man and its dependence on the structure and creation of the world. Indeed, the first chapter of his *Ethical Discourses*,[4] entitled "A partial physiology of the creation of the world and the formation of Adam," is a classic text for the Orthodox view of man and the world. There he stresses that man comes into contact and communication with the world through his senses. But while the senses inform man of the beauty of the world and the grandeur of created things and of God's creation as a whole, at

2   Gen 2:7.
3   1 Cor 15:47.
4   SC 122.174-184, lines 1-146; *On the Mystical Life*, vol. 1, 21-26.

the same time they express man's unreasonable demands and his unnatural attitude to creation. This happens when his relationship to the world is not a personal one, but a projection of his biological individuality. Thus the unquenchable thirst of the senses for absolute pleasure is the tendency of physical individuality in a state of revolt to become an absolute, an end in itself. This, however, is a state contrary to nature. This is why the experience of the world and its beauty provided by the senses does not correspond to the truth of the world and its loveliness, but to the hedonistic demands of the senses. The result of this tendency on the part of the senses is a distortion of the beauty of created things, their degradation to such a level that they do no more than to serve man's gluttony and delight his senses.[5]

The anthropology put forward by Christianity is completely different from that of the ancient philosophers. It is a fact that behind this difference in the view of man lies a difference in the understanding of creation. As we said in the previous chapter, the ancient philosophical conception of creation—at least as expressed in Plato and the neo-platonists—accepts matter as eternal. Matter is not something which God created out of nothing, but something which already existed. Again according to this understanding, while it is possible for God to impose form and order on matter, matter remains totally outside God, as a second independent principle. Christianity, on the other hand, rejects any form of metaphysical dualism. According to the biblical understanding, matter is not co-unoriginate with God or independent of Him, but created by Him, as are the immaterial beings. The Book of Genesis relates that "God made the heaven and the earth... And God saw everything that He had made, and behold, it was very good."[6]

5 See Abba Isaac the Syrian, Letter 4, *Ascetic Works* (in nineteenth-century Greek translation), ed. Ch. Spanos, p. 389: "Contemplation of created things, though pleasant, is a shadow of knowledge, and this pleasantness is not totally separate from the fantasy of dreams."

6 Gen 1:1, 31.

Those who are eager on the basis of some of St Paul's Epistles
to find in Scripture some form of dualism and a hostily of the
spirit towards matter, should bear in mind that the word "flesh"
does not mean matter and the body, nor does the term "spirit"
mean the soul.[7] The word "flesh" simply means man in his fallen
state, while the word "spirit" means man in communion with
God. In consequence, it is possible for the soul to become
"fleshly," like the body; but it is also possible for the body to
become spiritual, like the soul. It is also characteristic that St Paul
does not exhort the Galatians to crucify the body, but to crucify
the flesh with its passions and desires.[8]

The Fathers of the Church, following the biblical anthropology, steered well clear of any sort of dualistic view of man. Even
when in some cases they seem to talk about the body in hostile
terms, it is understood that they mean the mind of the flesh.[9] This
is why they maintain that man is an unified psychosomatic whole:
"It is not a soul on its own or a body on its own, but the two
together that are and are called man."[10] The soul and the body
form parts of man, but not the whole man. The complete man is
the union of soul and body. Furthermore, the whole of Orthodox
theology highlights very clearly the importance of the human
body in God's plan of redemption, while at the same time showing us the potential offered by man's physiology for a foretaste of
good things to come even in this life.

Belonging as he does to this biblical and patristic line,
St Symeon the New Theologian maintains that in human physiology, the soul coexists with the body. "The belly, stomach and
apparatus of the intestines are the soul's intellectual workshop and

---

7   See Gal 5:19-21, where St Paul includes among "works of the flesh" dissensions,
    heresies and envy, which have no particular relationship to the body.
8   Gal 5:24. See also G. Mantzaridis, *Christian Ethics* (in Greek) (Thessaloniki, 1983),
    p. 328.
9   See for example Basil, *On "Look to thyself"* 3, PG 31.204C.
10 Irenaeus, *Against Heresies* 5.6.1, PG 7.1137A.

capacity for reception."[11] Man is a blend, a mixture, a creature formed together from matter and spirit, body and soul. It is difficult to isolate man's "spiritual stature" (or "maturity") from his body and to see it separately: "Thus we must add chest and back, shoulders, arms, hands and a neck to this body of spiritual maturity."[12] The body is the expression of man's personal existence. Man is body, and he gains the Kingdom of Heaven with his body.[13] Man's purpose and task is not to ignore his material nature, but to strive and struggle to use his body as a priceless gift from God. Man is positioned midway between the material and immaterial worlds. Because he participates in both simultaneously, he forms the bridge and point of contact for the whole of God's creation. Thus human nature, because it is a composite of matter and spirit, possesses greater potentialities even than the nature of the angels. Three centuries later, precisely this thesis will find its ultimate formulation and development in the teaching of St Gregory Palamas, who, far from regarding man as lower than the angels because he is a "mixture" of matter and spirit while they are "pure" spirits, goes so far as to maintain that man with his body is placed higher that the angels.[14]

In the consciousness and thought of St Symeon the New Theologian, man's material body is not there as an enemy which

11 *Ethical Discourses* 4, SC 129, p. 36; *On the Mystical Life*, vol. 2, p. 24.

12 *Ethical Discourses* 4, SC 129, p. 40; *On the Mystical Life*, vol. 2, p. 26.

13 See A. Keselopoulos, *Passions and Virtues in the Teaching of St Gregory Palamas* (in Greek) (republ. Athens, 1986), pp. 148f.

14 "For we alone of all created things possess the faculty of sense in addition to that of intellect and rationality," *Practical and Theological Chapters* 63, 150.1165C. On this theme in earlier patristic tradition, see for example the Areopagitic writings, *On the Divine Names* 4.27, PG 3.728D; Athanasius, *To Antiochus* 16, 28.608A; Gregory of Nyssa, Antirreticus 46, PG 45.1233Cc; *idem, On the Making of Man* 29.3, PG 44.236B, "So it is not true to say either that the soul is before the body, or that the body exists without the soul; but there is one principle of both, which in the higher sense is laid down in God's first act of will, and in another sense is constituted when the process of generation first begins." John of Damascus, *On the Orthodox Faith* 1.13, PG 94.853A.

has to be fought and conquered, but as a means whereby man has the capacity to glorify his Maker. It is especially characteristic that when referring to the body and the material part of man's nature, he very often speaks of the "temple of the body" and the "house of God."[15] So on this point too he is altogether in harmony with the teaching of St Paul, who insists that "your body is the temple of the Holy Spirit within you" and exhorts believers to glorify God "in their body and in their spirit, which are of God."[16] He is also totally in accord with other great Fathers who express the same doctrine based on the possibility of deification, which remains common to the soul and the body of man: "The whole man remaining in soul and body by nature, and becoming wholly god in soul and body by grace."[17]

Following the tradition of the Fathers before him on this point too, St Symeon maintains that the materiality of the human body did not prevent it from being incorruptible in man before the Fall: "Adam was created with an incorruptible body, though one which was material and not yet wholly spiritual."[18] But nevertheless, even in the present life, after the Fall, the human body achieves to some degree that incorruption which Adam had before the Fall, which will be the lot of all the righteous in the general resurrection at the Second Coming of Christ. This helps us to understand why the bodies of the saints are frequently preserved incorrupt after their biological death. It is the realization of the great potentiality given to matter and the body by the fact of Christ's Transfiguration on Mount Tabor, where His divine glory was manifested in and through His body. This is why the three

15 *Catechetical Orations* 30, SC 113, p. 204.
16 1 Cor 6:19-20; see also Rom 12:1, "I appeal to you therefore , brethren, by the mercies of God, to present your bodies as a living sacrifice, holy and acceptable to God."
17 Maximus the Confessor, *Difficulties*, PG 91.1088. See in this connection Gregory Palamas, *Defence of the Holy Hesychasts* 2.2.9, *Writings*, ed. P. Chrestou, vol. 1, pp. 514-5.
18 *Ethical Discourses* 1.2, SC 122, p. 184; *On the Mystical Life*, vol. 1, pp. 26-7.

disciples saw with their material eyes that "in Him the whole full-ness of deity dwells bodily."[19] Precisely as the glory of Christ is not only interior, but matter and His body are glorified too, so the same happens with the glory of the saints: their transfiguration emphasizes that man's sanctification and deification does not involve only the soul, but embraces the body as well.[20] Again, all the examples of physical glorification in the saints, those signs and foretastes of the ultimate general resurrection of humans with the body, underlines the great potential which the Maker has afforded the nature of the human body, a potential which defines this incorruption not simply as something "to come," but as something already inaugurated and being realized. If we wanted to borrow the words of St Gregory Palamas, we could say that "if the body will in the future partake together with the soul in the ineffable good things, then it is evident that it will so partake even now, as far as its capacity allows."[21]

From the physiology of the body, which is particularly strik-ing, St Symeon often passes to the physiology of the soul, making use of elements of the one which explain states of the other, and he underline the needs and expressions which they share. Thus when he talks about the value and importance of godly mourning and tears, he accepts that these are expressions of man's nature: "tears and weeping probably come naturally to man's nature."[22] In order to show that "it is a natural property of us all to weep," he refers to human birth, where the baby's cry is awaited by the mother and the midwife as a sign of life. But this crying shows at

19 Col 2:9.
20 "The body is deified together with the soul according to the participation in deifica-tion appropriate to it," Maximus the Confessor, *Gnostic Chapters* 2.8, PG 90.1168A.
21 *Hagioretic Tome*, PG 150.1233C. (This text is translated under the title "The Decla-ration of the Holy Mountain in Defence of Those who Devoutly Practise a Life of Stillness" in *Philokalia* IV [tr. G.E.H. Palmer, Philip Sherrard and Kallistos Ware; London, 1995], pp. 418-425.)
22 *Catechetical Orations* 29, SC 113, p. 182. In this connection see also Gregory of Nazianzus, Hom. 19.7, PG 35.1049D-1052A.

the same time that from the moment of birth, man's nature has as its "concomitant" mourning and tears. Precisely because the tears at birth are "indicative" of the tears throughout man's life, he should live this present life in that mourning and die with it, if he really wants to be saved and to pass into the true and blessed life. For just as food and water are basic essentials for the body, so the tears of godly mourning are essential for the soul.[23]

In the writings of St Symeon, which evince a marked anti-dualistic character, it is stressed that the body and its needs should not be belittled because they are material; there needs to be a proper attitude towards its materiality, as there should be a corresponding attitude towards the needs of the soul.[24] Just as the body without the soul does not move in any direction, so also the soul does not remain unmoved towards the desires and appetites of visible and non-sinful things and passions, even when it is in a union of love with God.[25] For in giving man materiality, far from putting obstacles in his way, God gave him the possibility of becoming more perfect. This, furthermore, is why neither the materiality of his nature, nor his nakedness, nor even the difference of sexes affected his state before the Fall.[26]

Man as a psychosomatic unity plays a central and decisive role in the world. This role does not concern only the world which we apprehend with our senses, but also the world of things which we apprehend with the intellect. Thus man becomes the locus for the encounter and interpenetration of the two worlds. Because he has senses, he participates in the material world around him, and this

23 In saying this, Symeon is taking up an exhortation from the teaching of his spiritual father, Symeon the Studite. See *Catechetical Orations* 29, SC 113, p. 184.

24 *Catechetical Orations* 26, SC 113, p. 82: "For since you are twofold, that is to say, composed of soul and body, you should take your food and meals in an appropriately twofold way; having a sensible and earthly body, you should nourish it with physical foods from the earth, and bearing an intellectual and divine soul you should nourish that with the intellectual and divine food of words."

25 *Catechetical Orations* 25, SC 113, p. 58.

26 *Ibid.*

world expresses itself and is apprehended through the senses. But because he also has an intellect, he is able to participate in the spiritual world. In the physiology of man put forward by St Symeon the New Theologian, intellect and senses coexist in man in a "Chalcedonian" synthesis. The body is intermingled with the immaterial intellect "without mingling" and "without confusion," while the intellect and soul "bring forth the immanent word" "unmixedly" and equally remain "without separation," "without change," "without confusion."[27] On the other hand, material parts of the human body such as the lips, tongue, teeth and vocal chords "clearly form articulate speech *by the spirit*." Thus man is presented as that rational and living creation of God's which came into being "by a mingling of opposites."[28]

Particularly "apophatic" and "Chalcedonian" is St Symeon's view of man, as formulated in many of the holy Father's writings. Man, he underlines, is a "rational animal" made up "ineffably" of two natures: the visible and sensible nature of the body and the invisible, rational and intelligible nature of the soul. Being "two-fold, from two natures," he is in a remarkable way situated in the middle of the entire creation, and as the frontier between material and immaterial creation he is situated between material beings and angels. We see in man the paradoxical phenomenon of his

27 "How is the flesh mingled with the immaterial intellect without mingling, without confusion,
How do the intellect and soul bring forth unmixedly
the immanent word within us, and remain the same,
without separation, without change, without confusion in anything?"
Hymns 31, SC 174, p. 396.

28 This synthesis is particularly striking in the following hymn of Symeon's:
"How is it, tell me, that from clay, the bones and sinews,
The flesh, the veins, the skin, the hair,
The eyes and ears, the lips and tongue,
The vocal organs, and the hardness of the teeth
Form clearly by the spirit speech articulate?
From matter dry and matter moist, from hot and cold
He formed me as a living thing, by a mingling of opposites."
Hymns 31, SC 174, p. 394.

existing as "immaterial" among sensible things and as sensible and material among the immaterial beings of creation.[29] In man's natural state intellect and senses—which constitute two elements—are interdependent, since the intellect does not manifest its energies apart from the senses, nor the senses apart from the intellect.[30]

Characteristic is the fact that while St Symeon the New Theologian comes from the ranks of monastic Fathers of the Church and speaks for the Christian tradition in its monastic form, he is clearly opposed to the idea that the body is by nature evil or unrelated to the unfolding of man's life in Christ. And something more: he refuses to accept the devaluing of the body relative to the spirit, or of the senses relative to the intellect, but accepts a relationship of reciprocity and respect between these two elements in man. Man's task is to harmonize and unite these two worlds so as to be able to give them expression in a movement of worship and love for God.

Finally, this position is very close to the world and the civilization of Byzantium, in which it finds expression. For in the Byzantines' understanding, man is body and spirit, senses and intellect, participating in both simultaneously, and hence he is therefore able to fashion matter and give it shape, making it articulate. The music of a Byzantine troparion, the movements in worship, the stones and tiles of a church, the tesserae of a mosaic are matter that have obtained expression and a voice and take part in this doxology. It is the language and the echo of the harmony of the spirit within the world of matter. This may explain the decisive significance of mathematics—particularly geometry—in

29 *Hymns* 53, SC 196, pp. 218-20:
 "A rational animal, I am saying; man twofold, from two natures,
 ineffably...
 Strange wonder—in the middle of all things,
 in the middle of all creations, I mean.
 What then are these creations?"
30 *Chapters* 3.34, SC 51, p. 140.

Byzantine art and aesthetics.[31] Through all this God is praised, and His glory is revealed. But everything becomes articulate because it is able to be fitted into a rhythm; and none of this can happen without the participation of the human body, where intellect and senses, spirit and matter, can enjoy the relationship described by the theology of St Symeon.

2. Man as the image of God

When Orthodox theology speaks of man, it describes him as created "in the image" of God. This applies also to man after the Fall, who, "though he bears the marks of transgressions,"[32] does not cease to be the work of God's hands and continues to show that he was made "in the image" of God.[33] As we saw in the previous section, being "in the image" presupposes the human body as well, since man can reveal his gift and his character only as a unity of soul and body. Furthermore, it is the composite nature, "without mingling" and "without confusion," of man who unites within him the different components of creation, that made the Fathers speak of him as a "microcosm,"[34] a little universe, whose task and mission it is to work as an intermediary and unite together all things in creation so that everything is lifted up through him into harmony with the Creator.

God in Trinity is a unity and communion of persons. Being made in the image of the personal God, man is himself a person. The Fathers of the Church speak at great length about man's

31 See Gervase Mathew, *Byzantine Aesthetics* (London, 1964), p. 23.

32 Office of the Dead.

33 On the meaning and significance of "in the image" see I. Karavidopoulos, *"Image of God" and "in the image" of God in St Paul: The Christological Foundations of Pauline Anthropology* (in Greek) (Thessaloniki, 1964), pp. 21f.; P. Nellas, "The Theology of God's image in man" (in Greek), *Kleronomia* 2.II (Thessaloniki, 1970), pp. 295f.; G. Mantzaridis, "The Teaching of Gregory Palamas on the Deification of Man," *Palamika* (Thessaloniki, 1973), pp. 155f.

34 Cf. Maximus the Confessor, *Mystagogy* 7, PG 91.684D-685A; Methodius of Olympus, *On the Resurrection*, GCS, Methodius 2, 10, 2-3, p. 351.

personal nature, since he is the only one of all created things to exist within creation as a person. This is to say that humans do not exist as mere biological units, nor do they simply share in a common good which is life: as persons who share the same nature, they are in communion and relationship with God and with each other.[35]

Being in the image is not a privilege belonging to certain humans only, but a gift to the whole of humanity. Underlining this truth, St Symeon the New Theologian says that "the Holy Trinity, extending through all from the first to the last, as it were from head to foot, brings everyone together and attaches and unites and binds them to Itself, and in bringing them together makes them strong and impregnable... revealing Itself to each person and making Itself known as one and the same."[36] Precisely because the whole rational creation possesses the image, no human being is originally evil by nature, since on the one hand God is not a maker of evil works—everything was made by God "very good"[37]—and on the other He Himself is good not "at will and by choice" but "by nature and in truth." In consequence, God who is good by nature cannot but have created man, as His image, with a good nature.[38]

The meaning and content of the person as an image of God and of the whole of creation, which forms the basis for communion in

35 On the distinction between the personal relationships of humans and social cooper-ation among animals, or indeed the functional cooperation of the parts of a body, see N. Matsoukas, *op. cit.*, pp. 280, 386 n. 24.

36 *Chapters* 3.2, SC 51, p. 120. Underlining this point, Gregory of Nyssa remarks: "The image is not in a part of our nature, nor is grace in one element of what we see in man; but such a power is to be found equally throughout the race. It is a sign of this that the intellect is established in all in the same way: all have the power of thought and deliberation, and all the other things through which the divine nature is imaged in the creature made according to It... So the whole nature, extending as it does from the first to the last, is one image of Him who is." *On the Making of Man,* PG 44.185CD. See also G. Manzaridis, *Sociology of Christianity* (in Greek) (Thessaloniki, 1985), p. 182.

37 Gen 1:31.

38 *Catechetical Orations* 3, SC 96, p. 322.

the Church, is founded on trinitarian and christological dogma. In both cases, we have a highly developed concept of the person as the mode of existence for the nature, and as an unrepeatable particularity, which is not confused with the nature but remains the expression of it. Despite the separate hypostatic properties which distinguish them, the Persons of the Trinitarian God commune with each other, partaking in the common essence and common energy: "The three are God, for the Trinity is one God,"[39] for It remains "one in nature and essence."[40] Personal relation and common participation make up the trinitarian communion, in which "without the Spirit there will not be the Father, nor His Son;"[41] and where it is not simply that there is no distance or separation between the Persons, but it is precisely this communion of the Persons of the trinitarian God that makes it possible for one Person to be witnessed to and revealed and seen by Another.[42] This is also why the communion of persons in the Church exists to the extent that it is expressed and made up of members who are persons, whereas we have no communion—and, consequently, no image of God—where we do not have persons.

For precisely this reason, man, having been created in the image of the personal God and the personal Word, forms the created hypostasis of the "words" or inner principles of beings. Created by the God who loves mankind as "a natural bond, as it were" among all things, like a true "microcosm"[43] man sums up all created realities and receives the natural dynamism of creation, which he is called to lead to its end. By the fact of being in God's image, man is called by God to preserve and fulfil the right

39 *Hymns* 51, SC 196, p. 190.
40 *Hymns* 44, SC 196, p. 76.
41 *Ibid.*, p. 74.
42 "For the Father of the Son
      is in no way divided from Him,
      But in the Son is He seen,
      and the Son abides in Him." (*Hymns* 44, SC 196, p. 74)
43 Maximus the Confessor, *Mystagogy* 7, PG 91.684D-685A.

orientation of this dynamism. He will succeed in this task when he makes proper use of the gifts and physical powers with which he has been endowed by virtue of being in God's image. Man is an image of God in all the relationships in his life—personal, social, political, economic, ecological—and has the gift and also the responsibility of living "before the face" (or "person") of God, of living up to the word of God and bearing witness to the world of his mission as God's image. He is a person in the sight of God, and for this reason he is capable of conversing with God and is responsible before Him. And the natural consequence of his being made in this way is that his rights and his obligations as a human being are inseparable and indivisible.[44]

On the other hand, the Son and Word of God as person bears the divine nature as being "inseparable" from the Father and the Holy Spirit; yet once He takes flesh and becomes "what He was not," namely man, He bears human nature as well. The person of the incarnate Word remains one, since the two natures, the divine and the human, exist together—"seen by all as God and man together"[45]—and have a common expression in the person of God the Word. Thus the communion of human persons with Christ has as its basis and theological foundation the union of the two natures in the person of Christ, without change, without confusion, without division and without separation, and also the union and communion of Christ with the other two Persons of the trinitarian God. Expounding a passage in Christ's high-priestly prayer which refers to His relationship with His Father and with His disciples,[46] Symeon says that these words imply "the equality of their union with each other." The only difference is that the

---

44 On current thinking based on the theology of the image, see further J. Moltmann's study, "Theologische Begründung der Menschenrechte," *Politische Theologie-Politische Ethik* (Munich, 1984), pp. 166-179.

45 *Hymns* 51, SC 196, p. 190.

46 "Even as Thou, Father, art in Me and I in Thee, even so they may be in Me and I in them;" cf. Jn 17:21-23.

union of the Son with the Father is "by nature and has no beginning," while our union with the Son is "by adoption and grace." Nevertheless, as a communion of persons we are all able to exist in union with God and inseparable from Him and from each other.[47]

Our creation in God's image is also the basis for the tripartite division of the human soul accepted by most of the Fathers. Attempting to explain the mystery of man, they take as their basis and point of reference the Archetype of every reality, in whose image man is made. Thus after the manifestation and revelation of the Archetype which is God in Trinity, they use the method of psychological analogies in order to reveal and depict the content of the human person which is the image and likeness of God.[48] St Symeon the New Theologian talks at length about the existence and functions of the faculties of reason, appetite, and irritation in the "spiritual workshop of the soul."[49] In parallel, he notes the movements and assaults of the passions in each of the functions of the tripartite soul.[50]

On occasion, mainly through the influence of theological scholasticism in its various forms, attempts were made to enshrine a one-sided understanding which dictated that the phrase "in the image of God" should be understood as referring to the quality of man's spiritual and rational being alone—the very notion that has

47 *Catechetical Orations* 34, SC 113, p. 280. On the relationship of the Persons of the Trinitarian God, see also *Hymns* 44, SC 196, pp. 74f.

48 It is characteristic that when St Gregory Palamas refers to man, he speaks of his essence and energies (or powers), of his nature which is unified but at the same time trinitarian (intellect, reason, spirit). And when speaking of the trinitarian character of the soul he says that it is "that trinitarian nature after the Supreme Trinity, which has been made by It as an image of Itself more than other creatures, being intellectual, rational and spiritual." *Natural and Theological Chapters* 40, PG 150.1148C and *Demonstrations* 2.9, Chrestou vol. I, p. 85. On the use of psychological analogies in Palamas see Amphilochios Radovic, *The Mystery of the Holy Trinity according to St Gregory Palamas* (in Greek) (Thessaloniki, 1973), pp. 45f.

49 *Ethical Discourses* 4, SC 129, pp. 36f.; *On the Mystical Life*, vol. 2, pp. 24f.

50 *Chapters* 3. 63, SC 51, p. 158. On the tripartite nature of the soul and the appearance of the passions see A. Keselopoulos, *Passions and Virtues* (in Greek), pp. 55-66.

fomented the whole imbalance in man's relationship firstly with his body (i.e. with himself) and then with all the rest of "material" creation. But in spite of this, Orthodox theology, cosmology, and anthropology have not ceased to maintain that man is an indissoluble unity of spirit and body. St Symeon the New Theologian, as a true representative of this theology, speaks on this basis of the relationship between the material and spiritual elements in man;[51] while in another case, talking about man as the image of the trinitarian God, he underlines the indwelling of the uncreated in the created, which is the greatest honor and dignity bestowed by God on the "earthen vessel"—the human body.[52]

So when the Fathers of the Church talk about the image, they are referring to the whole of man's psychosomatic being. They do, however, use certain predicates to indicate the ontological difference between person and nature and to reveal the universality but also the dissimilarity of the person. Such predicates stress the elements of rationality, freedom, and rule.[53] St Symeon the New Theologian underlines the point that these three capacities with which man is endowed are thought of together and regarded as equally important, but at the same time are distinguished from one another.[54] If anyone wants to do away with one of these, he will of necessity do away with the others too, because it is by these three capacities of the image—which is man—that we are led to the Prototype who is God in Trinity.

51 See *Ethical Discourses* 3, SC 122, pp. 400-402.
52 *Catechetical Orations* 27, SC 113, pp. 108-110.
53 "In how many ways is man said to be in the image? In his capacity of being rational, possessed of intellect and having free will; in the fact that his intellect generates speech and his breath sends it forth; in his capacity to rule." John of Damascus, *On the Two Wills in Christ*, PG 95.168B.
54 "The three are one, in unity but also distinct.
      For ever they are united, and are separated;
      for they are united without confusion, divided up inseparably.
      Removing one of these, you have altogether removed them all...
      In this way, from the image you understand the prototype."
    Hymns 44, SC 196, p. 74.

So apart from his free will, man has been honored more than all other creatures with the rational faculty, through which he "rules and reigns over them." Through his own capacities he is meant to discern these gifts of God which testify to his creation in God's image.[55] St Symeon himself has a strong sense of the uniqueness afforded to man by his creation in God's image and likeness, as he has a strong feeling for the fact that man was created to function as king of creation.[56] His relationship to the rest of creation is in accord with this—as is that of all the saints and deified people. It is a purely eucharistic relationship, one of thanksgiving. Centuries ago, St Symeon and the Fathers spoke of man being placed in the world by God as king and priest. Today, man is beginning to realize what great power he wields, and to feel the need for wisdom and humility in the exercise of this power.

There were of course church writers, chiefly in the early days of the Church—and so in a historical environment not yet free from paganism—who refused to include the body in the image of God, since it was a matter of keeping the truth of God safe from any bodily and anthropomorphic analogy.[57] But the Fathers of the Church emphatically underlined many times that the image of God refers to man's psychosomatic totality and unity.[58] More

---

55 *Ethical Discourses* 2, SC 122, pp. 142-4.

56 *Thanksgiving to God*, Hom. 35, SC 113, pp. 304-6: "For You brought all things out of non-being for no other reason than for me, who am in Your image and likeness, having made me king of everything on earth to the glory of Your great work and Your goodness."

57 See Origen, *Against Celsus* 6.63, PG 11.1396A: "For if the image of God is in the body alone, then the better part, the soul, has been deprived of the image, and it is in the corruptible body, something that none of us says. But if the image of God is in the two together, then God is necessarily composite... so the image of God is left in what we call the inner man."

58 See Cyril of Alexandria, *Commentary on John's Gospel* 9, PG 74.277D: "To our own proper nature formed from two elements, I mean soul and body, the Maker affixed like a stamp of His own nature the Holy Spirit, that is, the breath of life, through which man was formed in accordance with the archetypal beauty and made in the image of the Creator, maintained in every kind of virtue by the power of the Spirit

often, however, patristic interpretations sum up the truth of the image in the trinitarian character of the personal energies which are expressed in the property of rationality (intellect, reason, spirit) or the properties of rule and free will, which above all summarize the creation of man in God's image in the differentiation of the person from the nature.

Specifically, St Anastasius of Sinai considers it "obvious" that the chief component of the image in man is "our soul, and its spiritual reason, and the intellect."[59] St Gregory of Nyssa underlines that "where there is the power of ruling, there is the image of God,"[60] while St Cyril of Alexandria emphasizes that as man has free will, he is a voluntary agent and is also responsible for curbing his desires; this too is a corollary of the image, since God "exercises authority over His own acts of will."[61]

St Symeon the New Theologian stresses man's superiority with his characteristics of rationality, rule, and free will, particularly in his life and his state before the Fall, when neither the division of the sexes into male and female, nor his nakedness, nor even the existence of the rest of material creation (foods and other material goods) around him "hindered either of them from chaste sobriety."[62] Finally, the qualities of rationality, rule, and free will are the main components of the image of God in man as regards his relationship with the world and creation, as we shall show.

3. Man in the world

We have seen that man as a product of nature sums up all the elements of the world. But since his fall and his choice of a life

dwelling in him." See also Irenaeus of Lyons, *Against Heresies* 5.6.1, PG 7.1137A, and Gregory Palamas, *Natural Chapters* 63, PG 150.1165CD.

59 *On the Image*, PG 89.1148BC.

60 *On the Making of Man,* ed. Hörner (Leiden: Brill, 1972), p. 16.

61 *Dissertation on John* 9, PG 74.277D.

62 *Catechetical Orations* 25, SC 113, pp. 56-58.

contrary to nature, these elements are in a state of fragmentation and division not only in man himself, but also in the world around him. Since, however, he possesses the image—albeit now grown dark—even after the Fall and remains a personal being, a rational psychosomatic hypostasis, he preserves the capacity to realize dynamically in his person the unity of the world; to sum up the "principle," the logos or "word" of the world in a personal answer to God's calling of the created to communion and relationship with the uncreated; and to offer up the "word" of the world as a personal "word" of the creature's praise to the Maker.

It is a commonplace in the teaching of the Church Fathers that man, as a summing-up of the created world and a small-scale version of it, is the *microcosm*, while the universe as a large-scale version of man is "macroanthropos." St John of Damascus calls man a microcosm because, having a soul and a body and being midway between intellect and matter, he is a bond between visible and invisible creation, between the sensible and the intelligible.[63] St Gregory the Theologian sees man, "this little world,"[64] "as a second world, a great world in miniature upon earth."[65]

The idea of the world being summed up in man is something we encounter also in ancient Greek thought as part of a moral outlook, as in Democritus,[66] or of a physical approach to the subject as in the writings of Plato[67] and Aristotle.[68] Yet the critical difference in the patristic view is precisely that it goes beyond the descriptive analogy and gives a dynamic character to the truth of man as *microcosm*, as is shown principally in the teaching of St Maximus the Confessor.

63 *On the Two Wills in Christ*, 15, PG 95.144B.

64 Hom. 28 (Second Theological Oration), 22, PG 36.57A.

65 Hom. 38, (*On Theophany*), 11, PG 36.324A.

66 See H. Diels-W. Kranz, *Die Fragmente der Vorsokratiker* vol. II, No. B34, p. 153.4-11.

67 See *Timaeus* 81a 2-b2 and *Philebus* 29b-30a.

68 "If this can happen in a living creature, what is to prevent the same thing happening throughout the universe? For if it happens in a miniature world, it will happen in a large one too." *Physics* IX 2.252b, 24-27.

This view of a correspondence between man and the world, as it exists in patristic thought and especially in St Maximus the Confessor, is adopted by St Symeon the New Theologian too. The world can be described "in miniature" in terms of man, while man can be contemplated "writ large" in terms of the world. Intelligible creation is the soul of the world and sensible creation is its body. In man, conversely, the soul is the intelligible creation and the body the sensible. The world stands as an image and type of what takes place within man. Taking images from the sun, the moon, and the other heavenly bodies, St Symeon applies them to man; and he underlines that the world as an image of man was not invented by human beings, but it was made that way by God Himself. The craftsman Word of God "sketched out in advance" in creation, as in a picture, everything that was to take place for the salvation of man; in order that man, seeing the picture revealed in sensible things, should be able to accept without doubt that within him, too, "the real truth is completed and perfected spiritually." Knowing that each man is a second world created by God, a "great world in this small and visible one,"[69] he should not show himself worse and more irrational than the dumb beasts or inanimate creations. For these were created by God who loves mankind for the instruction of man, who is obliged to try to imitate whatever good he finds in them and avoid by every means those characteristics unworthy of imitation.[70]

By his very makeup, man has the privilege of being on the borderline between certain divisions,[71] which he must overcome if he

---

69 *Ethical Discourses* 4, SC 129, p. 64; *On the Mystical Life*, vol. 2, p. 37. See also Gregory the Theologian, Hom. 38, 11, PG 36.324A and Nikitas Stethatos, *Contemplation on Paradise*, SC 81, p. 158, 3ff.: "The other [world], the intelligible and invisible, being within man; man who in the small, visible world is created for a great world, and on earth stretches out towards God."

70 *Ethical Discourses* 4, SC 129, p. 66; *On the Mystical Life*, vol. 2, p. 37.

71 Maximus the Confessor, for example, sees five such divisions: first, between created and uncreated nature; second, the division of created nature into sensible and

is to fulfil his natural destiny. This is seen more clearly in man's state before the Fall, when, as we have noted, neither the distinction of the sexes nor the existence of foods and other material goods presented any obstacle. On the contrary, the unifying of these opposites was a personal possibility and duty for him.[72]

The whole of material creation was given by God as a blessing and a gift to man. This is something that Symeon particularly stresses. Interpreting the relevant passage of Genesis (1:28), he underlines that God did not grant man paradise only, but the whole earth. "All things visible, those on the earth and those in the sea, He gave to Adam and to us, his descendants, for our enjoyment."[73] "Look up at the sky above and down at the earth," he says, "and understand what works God has made, and how many things He has made, all for us."[74]

The close relation between man and creation is stressed first of all in the Old Testament story which speaks of the creation of the world and of man. There it is said that "the Lord God took the man whom He had made and put him in paradise to till it and keep it."[75] Explaining this passage—and referring at the same time to man's spiritual life—St Symeon sees the "tilling" and the "keeping" as interdependent notions, referring to man's rights and also his obligations towards the environment in which he lives. A proper relationship with creation and proper exploitation of it, i.e. "tilling," necessarily also implies the duty of further protecting and preserving creation, the "keeping." What is the point of

intelligible; third, the division of things sensible into heaven and earth; fourth, that of earth into paradise and the inhabited world; and fifth, the division of man himself into male and female. On this see *Difficulties*, PG 91.1304Dff.; also L. Thunberg, *Microcosm and Mediator*, pp. 147-8.

72 *Catechetical Orations* 25, SC 113, pp. 56-8.

73 *Ethical Discourses* 4.1, SC 122, pp. 176-88; *On the Mystical Life*, vol. 1, pp. 21-26: "The whole world was given to Adam, just like a single country, or like one property."

74 *Catechetical Orations* 19, SC 194, pp. 322.

75 Gen 2:15.

sowing, he asks, if the seed is left unwatered and generally does
not receive the care it requires? It is impossible that it will be able
to germinate and grow and bear fruit, because either the thorns
will have choked it, or the birds will have eaten it. So a right use of
creation without at the same time protecting it is not possible.[76]
Moreover, the command to "till and keep" was given to man, who
is of course "of earth" since he comes from the clay of the ground,
but also has an intelligible soul, since he has received the breath of
life and has been created in God's image. It is characteristic that
this command is given to man in the context of his being "in the
image," which expresses man's free communion and relationship
with God. God places man in the world as His representative, in
order to exercise there God's care and providence, participating in a
continuous act of creation and guiding creation to its perfection.
For this reason, the degree to which man lives up to this command
also gives the measure of his communion with God.[77]

Here it should be emphasized that the notion of conserving
and protecting the world from ruin and disaster includes respect
as a primary element. Man respects the world when he is aware
that the world is a creation of God with a specific purpose which
is anterior to it. As a creation out of nothing, the world neither
had nor has the capacity to set a purpose for itself. The purpose of
the world is independent of the world; it is to be found in God.
But the world is not independent of its purpose and destiny. For
this reason, conserving the world means first and foremost conserving the purpose of the world. If man changes the purpose of
the world, he changes the nature of the world and distorts it;
while if he shifts its ultimate goal, then he destroys the world.

This truth is of decisive importance on the question of technology. If Scripture and the Fathers stand in general for a sensible,

76 Hymns 17, SC 174, p. 68. See also I. Galanis, "The Relationship between Man and
    Creation according to the New Testament," supplement 36 of Epistimoniki Epeteris
    Theologikis Scholis Thessalonikis, vol. 27 (Thessaloniki, 1982), p. 25.
77 Ethical Discourses 13, SC 129, p. 402; On the Mystical Life, vol. 2.

conscientious, and rational control over the environment, then this way of life presupposes a careful and environmentally responsible use of technology. Man's aim cannot be the rejection of technology, but the exercise of a more careful and humane control over it, so that it does not get in the way of the purpose and destiny of the world. Scientific research and development under certain preconditions, far from being harmful, are actually seen as essential in order to achieve and preserve a healthy environment. Pollution control, new sources of energy, recycling of waste, new construction materials and so many other good things in our technological civilization depend on the development of technological knowledge. For this reason, it is stressed today on many sides that man's mastery over nature has to be continued, with greater skill and wisdom than in the past. The slogan of a return to some pre-scientific civilization is today not merely a utopia, but may be a disaster for humanity. When man loses his ability to overcome nature, he does not attain to a true relationship with nature, nor does he preserve its purpose; he simply achieves a "vegetative" state. This word does not denote man's return to nature, but his identification with nature in the realm of decay and death.[78]

Through his senses, man sees in the sensible things of the world the ineffable gifts of God.[79] But in order to reach this point, he must first struggle to purify his senses.[80] Thus already in this world, on earth, here and now, man is able to participate richly in the grace of God: "those who participate richly in His grace, even

---

78 Indeed, when the term "vegetable" is applied to humans it denotes this state of death and moribundity. See T.S. Derr, *Ecology and Human Need* (Westminster Press, Philadelphia, 1975), pp. 43f. For further thinking on this whole subject, see for example P. Land (ed.), *Theology meets Progress* (Gregorian University Press, 1971), p. 57; J.-M. Aubert, *Pour une théologie de l'âge industriel* (Paris: Cerf, 1971), pp. 27f.; D. Dubarle, *Approches d'une théologie de la science* (Paris: Cerf, 1967), p. 15; D. Meadows, *The Limits of Growth* (New York, 1972), p. 175; E. Schumacher, *Small is Beautiful* (New York, 1973); H. Immler, *Natur in der ökonomischen Theorie* (Opladen, 1985); P. Reclam, *Ökologie und Ethik* (Stuttgart, 1980).

79 *Ethical Discourses* 3, SC 122, p. 402.

80 *Ethical Discourses* 3, SC 122, p. 408.

though they are present on earth..."[81] The perception of the Kingdom of God, far from being impeded by material things, is actually realized through them;[82] all that is needed is for man to
acquire in his life "a measure of spiritual knowledge."[83] Furthermore, in giving man a material nature and placing him in the
material world, so far from putting obstacles in his way God gave
him the greatest potential for perfecting his nature.[84]

Man received from God the authority to "subdue" or have mastery over the earth and to "have dominion" or rule over all the creatures of sea and land.[85] Man's mastery, particularly in the animal
world, is referred to also at another point in Genesis (2:19), where
God brings all the animals and birds before Adam "to see what he
would call them" and their names remained the ones they had
received from him. Naming is an action that indicates mastery.[86] In
giving names to living creatures, man is exalted above the other
creatures and stands as their overlord, and in consequence the overlord of all creation. He has dominion over the animals, as over the
whole of nature, as a creature in the image of God.[87]

Modern writers have picked up this special position which the
biblical tradition accords to man and seen it as the main cause
which has led man to the position of oppressor and embezzler of
creation. In reality, however, it is not this biblical teaching but its
misinterpretation and corruption that has led relations between
man and creation to this point. A glaring example of misinterpretation and corruption of the biblical tradition on this point is the

81 *Chapters* 1.3, SC 51, p. 40.
82 *Ethical Discourses* 3, SC 122, p. 412.
83 *Chapters* 1.33, SC 51, p. 58. See also Wis 13:5, "For by the greatness and beauty of
     the creatures, proportionably the Maker of them is seen"; cf. Rom 1:20.
84 *Catechetical Orations* 25, SC 113, pp. 56-58.
85 Gen 1:27-29.
86 This is attested also by the fact that God Himself gives a name to each thing after
     He creates it.
87 Gen 1:27;1:28. See I. Galanis, *The Relation between Man and Creation*, p. 26.

spirit and attitude that have taken the Western Christian world by storm from the Renaissance onwards. There man has been made autonomous; he has ignored God and placed himself as the absolute overlord and oppressor of creation. This is also the spirit of secularization, a state of affairs which par excellence encourages man to organize his life without reference to God.[88] And it is of course superfluous to stress that this arrogant attitude runs totally counter to the spirit of biblical teaching. As has aptly been remarked, "the whole description of creation [in Genesis] is at the same time a sermon against the pride of created things. The value of all created things is due to their origin in the creative work of God."[89]

The world, with its potential for incorruption while yet being material and sensible, is given by God to man "for enjoyment."[90] God creates man last as "king" of creation and offers him all the other creatures to serve him, even though all of them, "like servants," were fulfilling man's need.[91] But if man was especially honored by God relative to all the other creatures and as a result "rules and reigns over them,"[92] this does not mean that his relationship with the environment can be an oppressive one. God's command to "subdue the earth" does not constitute a passport to unrestrained and uncontrolled abuse and destruction of the natural environment. Man's mastery over nature brings with it corresponding responsibilities. The ultimate problem in the relations between man and creation is not who will "subdue" whom, but how man is to coexist in harmony with the other creatures of

88 See further A. Keselopoulos, "The Rape of Creation and the 'Alternative Solution'" (in Greek), in *Diakonia*, p. 500.

89 M. Rock, "Theologie der Natur," in D. Birnbacher (ed.), *Ökologie und Ethik* (Stuttgart, 1983), p. 76, and G. Mantzaridis, *Introduction to Ethics* (in Greek) (Pournaras, Thessaloniki, 1988), pp. 104-5.

90 *Ethical Discourses* 1.1, SC 122, p. 174; *On the Mystical Life*, vol. 1, p. 22. See also Anastasius of Sinai, PG 89.540-541 and 961-970.

91 *Hymns* 45, SC 196, pp. 104-6.

92 *Theological Discourses* 2, SC 122, p. 142.

God.[93] Furthermore, the notion of man's mastery in creation is not unrestricted. It belongs in the context of his ability to use the potentialities of creation properly, so that it helps and serves him. This entails an obligation on man's part to protect creation. As we have seen, "tilling" and "keeping" are interrelated notions.

When anything is said about a right relationship between man and creation in Scripture and the Church Fathers, however, there is a constant, an essential parameter which is always brought into play—the right relationship between man and God. The necessity for man to be aware that he is constantly dependent on God is always stressed. St Symeon the New Theologian underlines that the change in creation after the Fall shows that its principle is God. If man takes that into account, then he will recognize that if he is to change his attitude to creation, he must set right his attitude towards God.[94] Especially noteworthy is the phenomenon of creation's faithfulness to God—"for all things kept the commandment of this one God of all, and keep it still"—in contrast with man's ingratitude and faithlessness.[95]

The state of man in his fall, however, will be the subject of a later chapter. What concerns us here is the fact that the sensible world fulfils its liturgical ministry in the hands of man. Just as at creation the world awaits its ruler in the person of man and is subject to him, so in the return of all things to the Maker the world progresses alongside man. When man himself finds his destiny, which is to glorify God, he also leads the whole of creation to its destiny, which is equally to glorify God. As he sanctifies the temple of his being, man also sanctifies the temple of the entire world. Thus he transforms creation, making it sing the praises of the divine Majesty.[96] In this liturgical expression, man's relationship with creation and with the Maker enters that place where the

93 Hymns 44, SC 196, p. 72. See also I. Galanis, op. cit., p. 26.
94 Ethical Discourses 1.7, SC 122, p. 188.
95 Hymns 45, SC 196, p. 106.
96 See Hieromonk Gregorios, op. cit., p. 22.

celebrant priest, by the grace of his priesthood, is accounted worthy to see and to minister to the nature of God which accomplishes all things, inexpressible and unapproachable.[97]

This upward movement in praise towards God the Maker and "Creator of all things" through the beauty of created things is often underlined by St Symeon.[98] Through God's material creations, man is led with time "to a more perfect glory and transformation."[99] It is especially characteristic of St Symeon, who so extols the monastic way of life, that he accepts this right relationship between man and the world even amidst the interference of the world. He takes the view that the quality of man's relationship with God's creatures does not depend on where he lives, but on how he lives and on his attitude to God. As proof he refers to the existence of saints who even in the world were well-pleasing to God, putting the things of the world in their proper place in their relationship with God.[100]

Finally, in the relationship between man and creation it is not creation that leads man to God; it is man who, with his personal potential as *microcosm* and *mediator,* ultimately "makes creation word," *logos.* This task, which has its beginning in the natural possibility for man to meditate between God and the world and finds its fulfilment when man is deified and brings the world back to the beauty in which it was first created, when there is total interpenetration of created and uncreated—this task was not realized by the first Adam. But it found its realization in the person of the second Adam, in Christ, the first father of the "new creation."

97 *Hymns* 19, SC 174, p. 98:
"What man, become God by the grace of the Trinity,
    and counted worthy of the glory that is above, the first glory,
    could conceive of anything still more glorious
    than to celebrate the Liturgy and to see the supreme nature
    accomplishing all things, inexpressible, unapproachable to all?"
98 *Ethical Discourses* 2, SC 122, p. 146.
99 *Ethical Discourses* 1.1, SC 122, p. 178; *On the Mystical Life*, vol. 1, p. 23.
100 *Catechetical Orations* 7, SC 104, pp. 64-66.

3

Misuse of the World

1. The fallen world

The harmony in relations between man and creation is disrupted by man himself. With his fall and disobedience to God's command, he also makes a change in his attitude to the rest of creation. God's command was directly related to the use of the world and of creation: "You may freely eat of every tree of the garden; but of the tree of the knowledge of good and evil you shall not eat."[1] But because man did not keep God's command and did not behave properly towards the area and the environment in which he had been placed, he took the consequences of his attitude. These consequences are warned of before the Fall—"in the day that you eat of it you shall die"[2]—but they are expressed above all in God's words to Adam after the Fall: "...cursed is the ground because of you; in toil shall you eat of it all the days of your life; thorns and thistles it shall bring forth to you; and you shall eat the plants of the field. In the sweat of your face shall you eat bread till you return to the ground, for out of it you were taken; you are dust, and to dust you shall return."[3] In these words, what is underlined most strongly as the consequence of the first humans' disobedience to God's will is the disruption in the relationship between man and the rest of creation.[4]

---

1 Gen 2:16-17.
2 Gen 2:17.
3 Gen 3:17-19.
4 See I. Galanis, *Relationship of Man and Creation*, p.89.

This disruption in the relations between man and creation is referred to also in the New Testament, which lays particular stress on man's responsibility and liability for the situation which has been created and which has encompassed the entire creation. St Paul particularly underlines that creation was subjected unwillingly to vanity and servitude: "For the creation was subjected to futility, not of its own will but by the will of him who subjected it" (Rom 8:20). It is clearly apparent that there is mutual influence and interdependence between man and creation in their progress through time and history.[5]

With this biblical foundation, St Symeon the New Theologian sees a complete disruption in the natural course of things and notes emphatically that the enslaved state of creation is not a natural development for it. Creation is presented as a victim, because on account of man it has lost its position in the scheme of things and the rule it originally followed, even though its present condition is regarded by some as its natural state. For this reason, creation refuses to be subject to man once he has transgressed. Describing creation's attitude to man after the Fall, Symeon writes: "When it saw Adam leave paradise, all of the created world which God had brought out of non-being into existence no longer wished to be subject to the transgressor. The sun did not want to shine by day, nor the moon by night, nor the stars to be seen by him. The springs of water did not want to well up for him, nor the rivers to flow. The very air itself thought about contracting itself and not providing breath for the rebel. The wild beasts and all the animals of the earth saw him stripped of his former glory and, despising him, immediately turned savagely against him. The sky was moving as if to fall justly down on him, and the very earth would not endure bearing him upon its back."[6]

---

5   On the importance of this passage for our subject and the various interpretations it has been given at different times see I. Galanis, *op. cit.*, pp. 90f.

6   *Ethical Discourses* 1.2, SC 122, p. 190; *On the Mystical Life,* vol. 1, p. 29.

Thus the Fall, in its cosmic reverberations, spoilt and altered not only the original relationship between God and man, but also the relationship between man and the world. The hymnography of the Church often speaks of the fall of man as the cause of the fall and corruption of nature: "For Christ is born in the flesh, renewing the creation that was corrupted through evil transgressions."[7] The conclusion of this hymn ("corrupted through evil transgressions"), which has particular importance for us, refers quite clearly to the cause of the corruption in creation. The hymnographer, obviously influenced by St Paul's theology,[8] regards man as responsible for the fall of creation since he led it astray and brought it into corruption through his own transgressions. Another hymn, which appears to regard Adam as bearing prime responsibility for the "thoroughly corrupted creation," underlines: "... for behold, you come to give birth to the Master, who desires to renew in truth the whole creation once thoroughly corrupted by the transgression."[9] This is the same theological position as in the Old Testament, which says, "Cursed be the ground because of you..."[10]

In many of his writings, St Symeon the New Theologian stresses the difference between man's states before and after the Fall in relation to the world. Adam, he says, was fashioned by God with a body that was incorruptible—though nevertheless material and not yet spiritual—and was placed by God his Maker in an incorruptible world as an immortal king; and it was not only paradise that was the incorruptible world, but the whole of creation. But because man despised God's commandment and showed lack of trust in his

7   Services for the Nativity.
8   Cf. Rom 8:20.
9   Compline, Kanon Ode 9 (Greek use), 24 December.
10 Gen 3:17-18. On all this see I. Galanis' study, "The New Testament Foundation for the relations between Man and Creation in the Church's Worship," (in Greek), in *EEThS, Volume in Honor of Professor Emeritus Konstantinos Kalokyris* (Thessaloniki, 1985), pp. 391-393.

Maker, he was immediately "stripped of his incorruptible vesture and glory, and clothed with the nakedness of corruption."[11]

Creation, too, undergoes a corresponding change after the Fall. The earth and the entire creation shows itself corruptible. This change and alienation in creation, which also shows that its principle is to be found in God, in absolutely explicable. St Symeon underlines that it was quite justified that man, who had been brought to corruption and death by transgressing God's command, should have to live on an earth that was corruptible and subject to flux and likewise to eat corruptible food. "Since unrestricted pleasure, and an incorrupt and effortless way of life had led him to forget that every good thing had come from God, and had brought him to despise the commandment which had been given him, he was justly condemned to work the earth with effort and sweat, and to draw from it, as from some niggardly steward of an estate, his daily bread."[12] After the Fall, the earth remains unfruitful unless man makes an effort to work it, and on its own brings forth thorns and thistles, whereas when man toils over it "it provides its fruits in a manner proportionate to his needs."[13] In the context of the Fall and man's failure, the difference between the singleness of the human inner principle and the polyphony of the principle of created things manifests itself as a movement towards an unattainable end, a movement which misses its purpose, and for this reason alters the whole of life. It is a movement of change which appears principally as a destructive alienation of the entire world.

The commandment which the first humans were given in paradise did not tell them to avoid nature, but to approach material creation and work with it. At the Fall, what came first was a failure to be mindful of God's benefactions, this mindfulness being the starting point for "tilling and keeping" creation; and then

11 *Ethical Discourses* 1.2, SC 122, p. 184; *On the Mystical Life*, vol. 1, p. 27.
12 *Ethical Discourses* 1.2, SC 122, p. 188; *On the Mystical Life*, vol. 1, p. 28.
13 *Ibid.*

there followed the act of eating "of the tree which He commanded them not to eat," which resulted first in spiritual death and later in physical death.[14] Thus man in his fallen state forgot that he had been placed by God as "a perfect initiate" (or "overseer") "of the visible creation and an initiate also of the intelligible" and that he had been honored by the Creator. So "though he was held in honor, he became like the irrational beasts weighed down with burdens, and having become like them he remains so still, not being converted or being recalled or brought back to his original dignity,"[15] despite the gift offered to him by the economy of our Lord Jesus Christ, the Son of God.

Here St Symeon stresses that when man abused his natural powers, he did not only disregard God but was also led to disregard the reason for his existence. This view prevails among earlier Fathers too. St Maximus the Confessor underlines that man "thus becoming a transgressor and disregarding God," subordinated the intellective power of the soul to the senses. Thus he did not just become like the irrational animals, but even surpassed them in irrationality, because he changed his natural reason into something contrary to nature. So the more he tried to know visible things through sense perception alone, the more he tied himself up in ignorance of God. And the more the knot of this ignorance tightened, the more he tried to sustain himself with enjoyment of the material things he knew about. Finally, the more he tasted this enjoyment, the more he strengthened the passion of self-love which it spawns.[16] But the more he cultivated the passion of self-love, the more ways he invented for enjoying pleasure, which is at once the fruit and the goal of self-love.[17]

14 *Ethical Discourses* 2.7, SC 122, p. 372; *On the Mystical Life*, vol. 1, p. 109.
15 *Chapters* 2.6, SC 51, pp. 104-106.
16 Translator's note: "self-love" (*philautia*) has the sense of "mindless love for the body," leading to self-indulgence and pandering to the body's desires. Cf. Maximus, *Second Century on Love*, 59 and 60; *Philokalia* II, p. 75.
17 *To Thalassius*, PG 90.253CD. See also G. Mantzaridis, *Orthodox Spiritual Life* (in Greek) (Thessaloniki, 1986), p.99.

Man's relationship with the rest of creation was fatally wounded by the event of his Fall and his apostasy from God. Human abuse and violation of creation take place according to the measure of man's separation from God. Hence the transgression of God's command and above all the lack of repentance on man's part was what separated him from paradise, since in his fallen state his alienation directly affects the whole of creation. Referring to Adam's lack of repentance after the Fall, St Symeon the New Theologian says characteristically that the cases of Enoch whom God translated from earth to heaven,[18] and Elijah who was taken up in a fiery chariot,[19] show God's good pleasure towards these two people who, despite living after Adam and his descendants, showed obedience to the will of God. So He honored these two men by translating them from earth to heaven, He delivered them from returning to earth and suffering corruption in it, and He gave them longevity so that they would die later, or rather depart with the prospect of the change and transformation to come. Hence, as Symeon underlines, how much more sympathetically would God have dealt with Adam if he had not transgressed the commandment, or had repented after his transgression! What glory and honor He would have given him, and granted him to remain in paradise![20]

In the fallen state, the world loses its original meaning as an ornament and a creation of God[21] and becomes charged with a negative significance. Thus the New Testament writers frequently speak of the world as an evil desire in corruption and fallenness. St James in his Catholic Epistle says characteristically: "Do you not know that friendship with the world is enmity with God? Therefore whoever wishes to be a friend of the world makes himself an enemy of God."[22] It is in this sense that Symeon, too,

18 Cf. Gen 5:24.
19 2 Kings 2:11.
20 *Ethical Discourses* 1.2, SC 122, p. 192; *On the Mystical Life*, vol. 1, p. 30.
21 Translator's note: *kosmos*, "world," comes from *kosmeo*, "to order or adorn."
22 Jas 4:4.

interprets love for the world as a lust for sin.[23] But when he exhorts us to abhor the world and to hate "the things of the world," he does not in any way mean God's creation, much less other human beings. He does not even mean any of the things that can be useful to man and provide "sufficiently" for certain needs in his life. What he means by "the world" is a sinful and impassioned relationship with things: "What is the world? It is sin, and attachment to things, and passions."[24] It is the relationship to the world which, as we shall see later on, is under the influence of the world-ruler, the devil.[25] In this perspective, and given the fact of the Fall in man's life, there is no risk of mistaking it for an negative attitude to the world when Symeon maintains that relationship with and love for God and for the world are not compatible: "one who loves the world does not yet love God."[26]

The world, then, may become a negative influence on man's spiritual life. Yet this is not the fault of the world, but of man's wrong attitude towards it. While in this case the world is identified with that realm which is influenced by the devil, Christ rescues man "from the depths of ignorance and the gloom of love for the world."[27] When the world becomes the sphere of influence of the demons[28] who try to deflect "our godly purpose,"[29] then the holy Father recommends Christians to hate the world and regard all the things of the world as refuse in order to be able to progress towards that true goal of their life which is salvation and deification.[30]

23 *Catechetical Orations* 5, SC 96, p. 444. Cf. 1 Jn 2:15-17: "Do not love the world or the things in the world. If anyone loves the world, love for the Father is not in him. For all that is of the world, the lust of the flesh and the lust of the eyes and the pride of life, is not of the Father but is of the world. And the world passes away, and the lust of it."
24 *Catechetical Orations* 5, SC 96, p. 440.
25 *Hymns* 17, SC 174, p. 86.
26 *Hymns* 43, SC 196, p. 68.
27 *Ethical Discourses* 4, SC 129, p. 20; *On the Mystical Life*, vol. 2, p. 17; cf. Jn 2:1ff.
28 *Chapters* 15, SC 51, p. 48.
29 *Ibid.*, p. 52.
30 *Ibid.*, p. 50.

Frequently the devil tempts man personally, trying to lead him astray into listlessness, laziness, and cunningly perverted recollections which turn against God who made and formed all things. Most of the time, however, he does not operate only through his personal presence, but tries to attack man through creation, making God's creations autonomous in man's eyes.[31] Hence the way creation is dealt with and used by the Fathers—especially those called *neptic*, who practice the virtue of watchfulness—has the aim of cleansing the polluted creation and delivering it from the influence of satan, since they do not recognize his rights over any part of it.

In his writings, St Symeon the New Theologian enjoins banishing the demons from our life so that the world can once again become *kosmos*, an adornment. In this case, mindfulness of Christ enlightens the human mind and "banishes the demons."[32] Furthermore the theology of the Orthodox Church, far from rejecting the presence of demons and demonic activities in creation, speaks of them extensively—especially in certain services such as the Blessing of Waters. Orthodox hymnography is utterly consistent with the teaching of the New Testament, where it is quite clearly stated that the Word of God came "that through death He might destroy him who has the power of death, that is, the devil..." (Heb 2:14), and that "the reason the Son of God appeared was to destroy the works of the devil" (1 Jn 3:8). Orthodox soteriology cannot be understood without taking into account the work of the devil and the teaching of the Apostles and Fathers on the subject. Natural evil is there because creation groans under the power of the devil and is in bondage to vanity and corruption. Thus the reality of demons is not a myth as far as the Church is concerned. The blessing of natural elements such as water, and of the whole creation, has precisely this purpose: to free creation from demonic control.

31 *Chapters* 1.66, SC 51, p. 76.
32 *Chapters* 1.2, SC 51, p. 40.

The religious life of the ancient Greeks was directly bound up with the natural environment, since their whole lives, which were predominantly agrarian and pastoral, unfolded amidst nature. This dependence on their natural surroundings often led to an anguished search for the mechanism by which natural forces work so that they could dominate nature. But the non-rational view of nature, especially among the common people, resulted in the imaginary connection of the natural environment with demonic powers which humans had to neutralize, by subduing or propitiating them in order for their life to proceed smoothly and their daily labor to bear fruit. The Greeks saw nature as full of spirits, demons and gods, whose presence filled the mountains, forests, rocks, rivers, springs, the sky, the sea, and the whole of the natural environment.[33]

The belief in demonic powers prevalent in ancient Greek worship is accepted by Orthodoxy. The demons, however, are not divinities, nor do they bear any relation to the saints, whom Christians now invoke. For the Church, satan is not merely a negative idea of evil, but an active force.[34] He has whole legions of demons and unseen powers under his authority and remains a violent adversary of man and of God's work. He has become "god of this age"[35] and "prince of the power of the air."[36] All this must, of course, be regarded not in a dualistic sense, but as a consequence of the Fall and of the freedom of the spiritual beings, which God never violates.

Again, as we have stressed in an earlier chapter, it is not the devil who controls and governs the world, but God. Interpreting

33 See M. Nilsson, *Greek Folk Religion* (Greek translation I. Th. Kakridis, Athens 1979), p. 2, and Fr Georgios Metallinos, "Ecological Correspondences and Differences between Hellenism and Christianity—Their Attitude to the Environment" (in Greek), in *Koinonia* (Athens, 1985), vol. 4, pp. 496f.

34 See Protopresbyter John Romanides, *The Ancestral Sin* (in Greek) (Athens, 1957), p. 60f.

35 2 Cor 4:4.

36 Eph 2:2.

the well-known passage of John (14:30) where the devil is referred
to as "prince of this world," St Symeon characteristically stresses
that this does not imply any real authority—anything of the sort
would be a blasphemy, since, as the Gospel tells us, satan does not
have authority even over swine.[37] Rather, it is our God and
Master, as Creator and Maker of all creation, who "rules with
authority and by nature" over all things in heaven and on earth
and under the earth, being Lord of all, both things that now exist
and those we shall see in the age to come.[38]

The devil works in creation as a parasitic force. For this reason,
the so-called natural world is not at all natural, since it is not in
the original state in which it was created, but in a state of fall and
rebellion, which leads to corruption and death. Outside this context it is impossible properly to understand St Symeon's position
as described above, or even indeed the services and prayers of the
Church which talk about delivering the world and creation from
the influence of the powers of the devil. In consequence, creation
since the Fall is not demonic, but its disrupted relationship with
man is what deprives it of its natural center and alters it. However
we understand the Fall, it is clear that we are dealing with a tragic
event, a primeval drama with direct repercussions in man's life
and also in his relationship with the rest of creation.

St Symeon the New Theologian emphasizes this truth, saying
that in the case where man in not aware of the gifts and good
things that God gives him, he is living in a state of misery and
hell. But in order to perceive the gifts of God through the world
and through sensible things, one needs to have true love for God,
for other people, and for the whole of creation. In the final analysis, the holy father continues, this is the tragedy of our life since
the Fall: that while we were created by God immortal and called
to be partakers and heirs in the Kingdom of Heaven, co-heirs

37 Cf. Mt 8:30ff.; see above, p. 32.
38 *Ethical Discourses* 11, SC 129, p. 370-2; *On the Mystical Life,* vol. 2, p. 148.

with Christ and citizens of heaven, we do not want even to perceive all the good things we have received from God.[39] So as the iron that is put into the fire or the inanimate skin that is dipped into the red dye feels nothing, in a similar way we who are in the midst of the many good things of God's creation have no perception of them, and do not glorify God or confess all his benefactions. Ultimately, man's alienation in this case makes him like the harlots who, having lost their natural beauty, "stupidly think to adorn themselves with makeup and paints foreign to them."[40]

All these things are consequences of the Fall. Since the Fall, man does not exist in his natural state, but in a state contrary to nature.[41] From this point of view the Fall can be understood as an unnatural state which has arbitrarily interrupted the upward dynamism not only of man, but also of the entire creation. Man in his freedom has put a barrier in the way of creation's movement and changed the goal of the world, transferring it from God to himself. So instead of bringing to completion the progressive creation of the world, man has corrupted it, because he has not developed it by a conscious effort or even protected its purpose, functionality, and order. But the rest of creation, which groans and travails with man on account of his fall, also participates in this state of corruption and unnaturalness. At the same time, however, it waits patiently for the sons of God to sanctify its inner principle in order that it may sing in praise of the Divine Love; in other words, it "waits with eager longing for the revealing of the sons of God." It waits to return itself, together with the sons of the Kingdom, into the hands of the Maker where is was born and whence it had its beginning. It waits "in hope that it too... will be set free from its bondage to decay and obtain the glorious liberty

39 *Catechetical Orations* 8, SC 104, p. 92.
40 *Ibid.*
41 See further A. Keselopoulos, *Passions and Virtues* (in Greek) (republ. Athens, 1986), pp. 29f.

of the children of God."[42] The fulfilment and realization of this waiting will be the subject of the chapters that follow.

2. *The world and matter made autonomous*

If a right attitude towards God entails right behavior towards creation and a harmonious coexistence with it, it can easily be understood why the Fall leaves a decisive mark precisely on man's behavior towards creation and has a fatal effect on his relationship with it. While after the Fall we have a deviation from the will of God on man's part, the rest of creation does not change course, but faithfully follows the laws of its Maker. This situation receives further expression when man makes creation autonomous, which leads ultimately to disharmony in his relations both with God and with creation itself. Regarded autonomously, the natural world is taken to be divine in itself. Yet the natural world is completely different from God. God transcends the world and the world takes its existence from God, because it is the creation and work of God.[43] This does not of course mean that the world has no value. But its value is not autonomous, but rather extrinsic and derivative. It is due to the fact that it was created by God. The world is "good" (Gen 1:8) because God created it; and "everything created by God is good."[44] Man's ascription of autonomy to the creation goes so far as to create a mythology around it and worship the creation "rather than the Creator" (Rom 1:25). This is ultimately the state of idolatry, which expresses a negative attitude on man's part towards God. If man remains in this state, he does not deny God only, but even his very self, since God is an element in man's being by reason of man's creation in the image.

On the other hand the dynamism of creation, having been arbitrarily cut off by man and restricted to creation itself, loses its

42 Rom 8:19ff.
43 Ps 8:4 and 18:2.
44 1 Tim 4:4.

natural movement towards the infinite God. For this reason it runs into blind alleys, frequently becomes destructive and often gives rise to phenomena which seem perverse and senseless: this is what we characterize in history as natural evil or chance. What has happened with the world is that it has become as destructive as a motive force which has lost its natural direction and function. The upward movement of creation has not been destroyed—man is not able to destroy what God has created—but it has been affected by corruption and turned into a mere alternation and cyclical movement, ending inevitably in death, where man and his works are henceforth imprisoned. This is what the Church Fathers call a state contrary to nature.[45]

This is equally the basis on which St Symeon the New Theologian treats the subject, regarding the autonomous status of material goods as an unnatural state both for man and for nature itself.[46] As he underlines elsewhere, people who do not have a right relationship with creation are as it were outside the world, living a life contrary to nature:

> Those with eyes do not look; having sight, they do not see
> nor are they able in the mind's perception
> to comprehend God's wonders, but are outside the world,
> or rather, they are in the world as dead, even before death;
> dwellers in nethermost hell even before they go hence.[47]

It is ultimately that relationship which obstructs the manifestation of the Maker's work through the creation. For nature, when it is rightly regarded as something created, becomes the ideal "conductor" through which man can apprehend the creative energy of the personal God and also His hypostasis, as He operates out of love and with wisdom. St Paul goes so far as to underline that those who do not believe in God even before Christ's

---

45 See P. Nellas, "Christians in the World" (in Greek), *Synaxi* 13 (1985), p. 13, and A. Keselopoulos, *Passions and Virtues,* pp. 23ff.

46 *Chapters* 1.42, SC 51, p. 62.

47 *Hymns* 32, SC 174, p. 402.

coming into the world are without excuse, because through idolatry and nature religion they have replaced God with His creature in order to satisfy their appetites and desires. Specifically, he writes: "Because God has shown it to them; ever since the creation of the world His invisible nature, namely, His eternal power and deity, has been clearly perceived in the things that have been made."[48] When creation is made autonomous by man in this way—when it is worshipped "rather than the Creator," which St Paul talks about further on[49]—this has as its direct result not only idolatry, but also the disruption in relations between the sexes, since the lack of proper respect for nature and matter has a direct impact on every one of man's personal relationships, and particular repercussions for every relationship to do with race and gender.

The act of making creation and material goods autonomous cannot be explained as true love for these things. When man makes creation and material goods autonomous from their Creator, he is living in an impassioned state. He is living in subjection to the material world, not because he desires and loves it in the right way, but because he has perverted his will and distanced it from God's life-giving energy. Again, man does not make matter autonomous because he has something of matter himself—because he is created from matter too—but because he is wrongly placed in relation to it. Furthermore the devil, who is the father of sin and the instigator of all passions, is operative and active in this area, without himself bearing any relation to the material and sensible world.[50] The possibility of free will in the devil and those who follow him allows for the perversion of the true love for matter and the world, ultimately ending in passions and sin. In this case, love for matter and creation is set in reverse motion to love for God, while correspondingly the man who is a "lover of matter" cannot be a "lover of God."

48 Rom 1:19-20.
49 Rom 1:25.
50 See A. Keselopoulos, *Passions and Virtues*, pp. 67f.

When the world is regarded as autonomous and cut off from the energy and grace of God, then it becomes "deceitful" and man lives in the vortex it creates.[51] In this state, he makes absolutes of things temporary and transient; he is unable to evaluate the sorrows and trials of life in the proper way and is worn out by misfortunes, while he delights in pursuing luxury and wealth. Thus he comes to be "an enemy opposed to God" since the morbid friendship of the world and "worldly effort" becomes enmity towards God,[52] and since material goods, once they are made autonomous, "are obstacles to love for God and to being well-pleasing to God."[53] When the world is made autonomous and cut off from its cause, which is the One God and Creator, it essentially ceases to exist: it is reduced to a state of non-being. This is why, as with the passions, one cannot talk about ontology but rather about phenomenology. St Symeon says that the world in this state—meaning, essentially, when man has this attitude towards it—is not among things "stable" but among those "in flux."[54] Because, as he himself underlines further on, this world as a work of God is one thing, but quite another is "the deceit of life and its supposed happiness" into which man is led by an attitude of abuse of the world.[55] The distinction between these two states is crystal clear in the holy Father's thinking.

Nevertheless, the theology of the Fathers never knew the principle of philosophical dualism, with its tendency to make separations, in the sphere of anthropology. Man is matter and spirit, body and soul united. There is no such thing as a human being without material substance. The resurrection of the dead and their appearance at the Second Coming will be include the body. Man is body, just as he is spirit. The notion of being "bodily,"

51   *Catechetical Orations* 2, SC 96, pp. 264-6.
52   Cf. also Jas 4:4.
53   *Catechetical Orations* 2, SC 96, p. 266.
54   *Catechetical Orations* 2, SC 96, p. 274.
55   *Ibid.,* p. 276.

referring to man's material substance, must not be confused with that of being *psychikos*, "natural" or "unspiritual" (cf. 1 Cor 2:14), which refers to the carnal mind. The former is God-given from man's creation, while the second is a deviation from the way he was created. It is also characteristic that when Scripture talks about the deviation, it does not use the terms "material" or "bodily," but principally the term *psychikos*, which denotes a wrong use of material things or of the body as autonomous, and in general an opposition to the order of the spiritual-material creation.[56]

Only with these preconditions, then, and given that man has made material goods autonomous and fostered the carnal mind, do the Fathers talk of the priority of caring for the soul which is and remains eternal, and of a corresponding contempt for the flesh which passes away.[57] Only in this way is it possible to understand what St Symeon the New Theologian says about the world and matter in relation to man's immaterial soul.[58]

When nature and matter are made autonomous, this principally reveals an inclination on man's part to dominate them. Misinterpreting God's original command to "be fruitful and multiply and fill the earth and subdue it" (Gen 1:28), man ends up exploiting nature and prostituting it at whatever cost so as to achieve material domination by force. God's words to the first-created humans have a different meaning, however. On the one hand, these words are spoken in view of the Fall; they have to do with overcoming the dangers that came from nature, after the Fall and at a period when man's life was under threat from the animal

56 See 1 Cor 2:14.
57 See for instance Basil, *On "Look to thyself,"* 3, PG 31.204C: "Disregard the flesh, for it passes away; take care for the soul, a thing immortal"; this certainly does not mean that St Basil or the other Fathers are introducing any form of dualism.
58 *Hymns* 28, SC 174, p. 300:
"Why do we look to things material, all these that decay,
having a soul immaterial and all immortal?"

kingdom. This is underlined by the second half of the verse, "and have dominion over all the beasts and every creeping thing...". On the other hand, it is also indicated through these words that God as Creator is represented by man, who looks after creation, as is also apparent from the scene where Adam is called by God in an anthropomorphic fashion to name the animals in Paradise.[59]

This tendency on man's part to dominate creation in a way contrary to nature, expressed in his making it autonomous, has as a direct consequence man's attempt to remove God from the world and confine Him to "heaven," to a realm ultimately alien and distant from that attainable in human experience. Thus the field remains open for man's dominance in nature and more generally in history. Man interprets the world and subjugates it to his individual intellectual ability. The world, which is regarded as an object—as something lying outside man and over against him—is organized in a rationalistic way, with a view to serving the autonomy of human needs and desires.[60]

This attitude, on which the whole phenomenon of modern technology is manifestly founded, regards creation and matter as autonomous and for this reason ends up making them absolutes and deifying them. In an exceptionally characteristic and revealing way, St Symeon the New Theologian underlines that when humans are in this state, they ultimately forget and ignore the God who made them and worship as gods not only idols and demons, but even the inanimate and irrational creation given by

---

59 Gen 2:20. In an earlier chapter of this study, we discussed the significance of naming in the Hebrew tradition.

60 On this phenomenon see further (all studies in Greek) A. Gousidis, *Church and Society*, (Thessaloniki, 1982), pp. 72f.; Efthymios Stylios (Bishop of Acheloos), *The Modern Urban Environment as a Pastoral Problem*, (Athens, 1980), p. 31; Hieromonk Athanasios Jevtic, "The Environment and the Person," in *A Study on Dostoevski* (Imago, Halandri, 1981), pp. 53f. On the reverse of this phenomenon, the outcome of a right attitude towards "Creator and creations," see Ioachim-Kimon Kolyvas, "The Orthodox Perspective in the Work of Papadiamantis," in *Diavazo* 165 (Issue dedicated to Alexandros Papadiamantis), Athens, 1987, pp. 80f.

God to serve them. Having given themselves over to every debauchery and impure act, they go on to prostitute and defile the earth, the air, the sky, and all the things of God's creation. For nothing else at all so defiles and befouls God's pure work as deifying it and worshipping on equal terms with God, which is a worship "contrary to the Maker and Creator," a worship without reference to God.[61]

Furthermore, regarding creation in a one-sided way deprives it of the essence of its purpose and leaves it a prisoner to the limitations of the spirit of fallen man, for whom its usefulness is based on external relationships which are created and maintained only by means of the objective material world and human logic. Such relationships are evaluated through an effort to understand the purpose of man's relations with objects, or on the basis of moral ends, laws, etc.[62] Any perspective of this sort indicates at the same time an arbitrary interruption of the upward dynamism of creation towards its Maker. And this constitutes in the final analysis the original sin, whereby man has placed a barrier in the way of creation's natural dynamism, the aim of which was to contribute to "the progressive elevation of the world from the lower to the highest, right on to the ultimate point of its destiny."[63]

In setting up such a barrier to the upward movement of creation, as we have said, man transfers the goal of the world from the infinite and eternal (God) to the limited and temporal (himself).

61 *Ethical Discourses* 1.2, SC 122, pp. 192-4; *On the Mystical Life*, vol. 1, p. 30.

62 See N. Nissiotis, *Prolegomena to Theological Gnoseology* (in Greek) (Athens, 1965), p. 63, and D. Staniloae, "The World as Gift and Sacrament of God's Love," *Sobornost* 5:9, 1969, pp. 664ff.

63 See P. Nellas, "Christians in the World" (in Greek), *Synaxi* 13 (Athens, 1985), p. 10, where he gives a footnote clarifying the essential premises for this argument, and says characteristically: "Being powerless on its own, [the world] becomes powerful when it functions as the created 'receptacle' of the uncreated Providence of God. Being infertile and absolutely incapable of bringing forth on its own anything on a level that transcends it, it becomes capable of doing this when it is fertilized by the creator Word and the life-giving Spirit of God."

This is the most destructive ultimate consequence to follow once man makes the world autonomous. Losing sight of the infinite and eternal God, he has imprisoned himself within the confines of creation, in the mundane state. The majesty of a world which he received from his Maker from the beginning and which by grace has within its nature the purpose and the possibility of coexisting with the infinite, is replaced with a myopic, positivistic admiration for a limited "space." This is what makes St Symeon the New Theologian underline that the world is to be looked at through its Maker, since making it autonomous and worshipping it "rather than the Creator" spells its corruption and destruction.[64] The Christian's affirmation of material goods must necessarily be placed in the perspective of the Kingdom of God. If these are "given independence" or made autonomous in any way, this is a deviation from the purpose of their creation.[65]

Making creation autonomous, as a form of self-affirmation on man's part, was the starting point which would lead to the construction of an anthropocentric world-image, a humanism which sees in the human microcosm and its "inner life" the possibility for intellectual and mechanical dominance over the "macrocosm" that is the rest of creation. The truth about man as microcosm, at least as conveyed by Western thought and theology, was understood in the context of mental conception, physical observation, coldly detached experiment and quantifiable relations.[66] When knowledge of the world departs from its Orthodox presuppositional framework, which always requires the world to be looked at through man's relationship with the Creator, it is made autonomous and acquires its own structure and organization; and this is no longer expressed in the significative terminology of aesthetic

64 *Ethical Discourses* 1.2, SC 122, pp. 192-4; *On the Mystical Life*, vol. 1, p. 30.
65 *Catechetical Orations* 2, SC 96, pp. 254-6.
66 M.-D. Chenu, *La théologie au douzième siècle* (Paris: Vrin, 1966), pp. 41-49 and 314; ET *Nature, Man and Society in the Twelfth Century* (Chicago and London, 1957), 33-48.

consideration or of theological interpretation, but in an objectively articulated scientific method, which is supposedly able to predict and account for what happens in nature.

Here it should be stressed that in most cases, what happens first is that the "value" of man is made autonomous, and this has the consequence that everything else can be made autonomous and independent. This form of autonomy, which arises from a one-sided and defective anthropology and a theological idealism, supposedly sees that man's supremacy relative to the rest of material animal nature is being threatened and tries to "reinstate" him by putting him in a position of splendid isolation from all other creatures. But the problem is created not so much by the emphasis on the especially exalted place of man within creation—something that Christian teaching also maintains—but principally by the devaluing and belittling of the other forms of life in nature which, according to this understanding, end up as mere inanimate materials for exploitation and exist only for the sake of man's material prosperity. The mistake is to see this state of affairs as having a basis in the superiority of man and the view that he is the crown of the whole creation. Especially today, any connection of this kind has destructive consequences for contemporary man's moral attitude towards nature and the environment. It is an attitude quite literally opposite to the Christian view of the whole creation, which stresses the moral obligation for man to show respect and loving devotion to the rest of creation.[67]

When man sees nature as God's creation, he does not risk falling into one-sidedness or ascribing autonomy from God either to himself or to the rest of creation. In the opposite case, when he gives absolute and autonomous status to himself or his qualities—his hard work, for instance—he deprives creation of its creative dynamism; whereas when he makes creation autonomous, he makes it an idol and falls into idolatry. St Symeon speaks at

67 Cf. N. Nissiotis, "Nature as creation" (in Greek), *Synaxi* 14 (1985), p. 16.

length about man's proper and healthy attitude to matter—as well as the wrong and morbid attitude—especially in his twenty-fifth catechetical discourse.[68] He stresses discernment as the saving grace in our attitude towards matter, material goods and creation in general. In matter—and, by extension, in the human body—there is nothing evil; all that is required is that matter should not be made autonomous and should not "revolt,"[69] but be rightly harmonized with the material-spiritual dimension of man and be placed in the proper theological and anthropological context.

3. Forms of abuse of the world

When the world is made autonomous from God, it loses its true dimensions. At the same time, man ceases to encounter the inner principles of things, (which will be discussed at greater length in the next chapter) as a manifestation of God's personal energy. With "utility" as the yardstick, the world is transformed into an impersonal object and violated unrestrainedly so as to be subjected ultimately to man's insatiable greed. This attitude, which is expressed in every-day actions and manifested in every aspect of life, goes beyond the bounds of use and constitutes abuse of the world, which is the greatest of sins. In an attempt to fill the existential void he has created by turning away from God, being at odds with his fellows and making creation autonomous, man moves on to activities strongly reminiscent of idol-worship.

Particularly characteristic of modern man is the attempt to use the intellectual and technical capacities (themselves treated as autonomous) which constitute modern technology to secure mastery over as large a part of creation as he possibly can, while interpreting and subjugating the world through his individual intellectual ability. It is quite apparent that he willfully ignores his

68 SC 113, p. 60.
69 *Ibid.*

"neighbor," who does not feature within the horizon of his ambitions. And perhaps something even worse: the complete annihilation of the other person comes as a natural consequence of this attitude towards creation and towards the whole of life. On the other hand, creation itself has been used by man in his autonomous state to develop various forms of idolatry. The substitution of worship of creation for the worship of God was at the same time manifested in the continuing abuse and distortion of creation, since creation was not regarded as a work of God's love which could be preserved and could fulfil its purpose only through man's love.

Whether we have a right attitude towards the world or abuse it is not, in the eyes of Orthodox theology, a mere detail: it is the touchstone for the whole of human morality. The Church Fathers insistently maintain that a person is characterized as virtuous or vicious according to his relationship with the things in creation and the way he uses them—either according to reason or contrary to reason—as this is manifested in his life: "for it is from using things with reason or contrary to reason that we become virtuous or depraved."[70] St Symeon the New Theologian regards as eucharistic that use of the world and enjoyment of material good things which is accompanied by praise of God, while he characterizes as sin the misuse of the world and participation in it without reference to the Creator. If man stopped at that use of all created things which is according to nature and kept "giving thanks to God who has made all things and given them to him," then, far from suffering any harm, "he would prosper far more."[71] By contrast, the transgression of God's commandment, which was a misuse of the world, was what caused man to lose the Kingdom of God, to be deprived of His glory and ultimately to die.[72]

70 Maximus the Confessor, *Chapters on Love* 1, PG 90.981B.
71 *Catechetical Orations* 5, SC 96, pp. 388-390.
72 *Ibid.*

This same choice of death, which is the ultimate "wage" of sin[73] as a way of life, has continued to this day to lead man to collective madness. The dire sickness of self-destruction which has broken out among humans particularly in recent years convinces increasing numbers of people that the problem is not just a scientific one, but above all a spiritual problem. The pollution of rivers, seas, and the atmosphere, the destruction of trees, the forests turned into lunar landscapes, the accumulation of radioactive residues in living creatures, the overloading of the atmosphere of our planet with carbon dioxide and all the other phenomena which testify to man's abuse and violation of nature, do show the inability of science to maintain the balance of the world—but beyond that, they also reveal first and foremost a profound spiritual crisis. Through sin, man has lost his direct and simple knowledge of the world—the knowledge which Adam had and which he was meant to bring to perfection—and in the midst of his general distraction and disintegration he now has various pieces of knowledge about the things of the world, fragmented, indirect, and permanently incomplete.

Furthermore, the inner insecurity which has possessed man since the Fall causes him to regard the environment with suspicion and fear and to see hostility in it. But the Fathers stress that the "hostility" of the environment has to do not so much with the destructive forces at its disposal, e.g. the presence of wild beasts, as with the deficiency in man's creativity and mastery due to the fact that he has turned away from God. Typical is St John Chrysostom's comparison of the situation with that of a slave, who commands respect among his fellow-slaves as long as he enjoys the master's favor; but once he loses that favor, he is afraid of everyone.[74] So man tries to impose his will on his environment according to narrow and self-serving criteria, while at the same time finding out with his constant interventions in the order of nature

73 Rom 6:23.
74 *Hom. On Genesis* 9.3, PG 53.78-9, and 14.5, PG 53.115ff.

that he is in danger from his own actions, which threaten him and war against him. His creative work turns into disaster for nature, the first victim being himself. We have a state of self-destruction which is accompanied, paradoxically, by the deification of creation and the elevation of the environment into an idol. A predatory attitude towards nature and the merciless exploitation of it has become a way of life, a norm. In this perspective, it seems natural and logical to go from unbounded exploitation of nature to harsh exploitation not only of other people but also of oneself.[75] The exceptionally dangerous way in which man affirms modern technology, which may cost him his very survival, shows the truth of this. The individualistic imposition of authority on the world and the attitude of consumerism, as these are served and secured today by technology on the one hand and by misguided economic notions on the other, constitute the practical application of a cosmology which accepts nature as an impersonal and neutral "datum" existing only to serve the desires and endless "needs" of humanity. It is therefore natural that St Symeon's cosmology, which is diametrically opposed to the modern view of the world, should reject the consumerist, *nouveau riche* spirit which exists today as a form of abuse of the world. He maintains quite bluntly that people who do not have a right relationship with created things are, as it were, outside the world, living a life contrary to nature. These are the people who are unable to understand the greatness of God's wonders in creation and who remain dead, carrying death around with their life on earth. Many of them make a fine impression in the eyes of other people, as "highly esteemed and rich and lording it over everyone" (to use a modern term, *nouveaux riches*)—the only thing they are unable to understand amidst the boasting, good living, and individualistic self-centeredness which possess them, is shame.[76] In this holy

75 D. Tsamis, "Man and the Environment in the Thought of the Three Hierarchs," in *Introduction to Patristic Thought* (in Greek) (Thessaloniki, 1985), pp. 204-5.
76 *Hymns* 32, SC 174, p. 402:

Father's writings the distinction is made crystal clear between use and abuse of the world. It is one thing, he points out, to partake of the world as the creation and work of God's love for man: quite another matter is "life's deception and its supposed happiness,"[77] in other words the acquisition and consumption of wealth, into which man is led by an attitude of abuse of the world.

The chief cause of this attitude towards the world and material good things is that man overlooks the great truth that creation was given by God for the common use of all people on equal terms.[78] It has now begun to be recognized that there is an organic link between environmental and social problems, which together grow out of the same ethical problem in modern man.[79] For instance, according to the findings of the relevant agencies of the United Nations and the European Community, the famines afflicting Ethiopia, Sudan, Mauritania and other African countries may have an immediate cause in drought and the rapid desertification of fertile expanses, but fundamentally they are due to impoverishment of the land connected with the monoculture of commodities to supply the consumer markets of the North. Thus we note the cynical phenomenon of reserves of dried milk being sent to dying children in Africa, while their own land, instead of producing traditional foodstuffs for local use, "is made barren by the monoculture of animal foodstuffs destined to feed

"For these indeed are they of whom Scripture speaks,
the highly esteemed, the rich, lording it over everyone,
who because of this believe that they are really something,
powerless to perceive their own shame."

77 *Catechetical Orations* 2, SC 96, p. 276.

78 Fr Dumitru Staniloae even speaks of "common ownership of creation" in his article "The World as Gift and Sacrament of God's Love," *Sobornost* 5:9 (1969), pp. 662-673.

79 See for example the study by J. Moltmann, "Theologische Begründung der Menschenrechte," in *Politische Theologie—Politische Ethik* (Munich, 1984), pp. 166-179, in which he attempts to place the ecological-environmental problem within the wider context of social and economic problems and to look at it in the context of human rights.

Europe's cattle."[80] Much the same attitude to the world and its
goods can be observed in the patenting of genetically modified
crops and the strong commercial pressures to open markets for
these crops, in spite of grave fears for the environmental and
social consequences of their introduction, particularly into poor
agricultural countries.

Yet the Fathers of the Church, many years before, underlined
the truth of equal rights in the use of material goods. St Symeon
the New Theologian says characteristically that all things and all
the wealth in this world are common to all people, just like the
light and the air we breathe, just as pasture on the plains and
mountains is common to the animals.[81] This theologian of our
Church gives the example of how animals use the good things of
creation, observing how much more irrational man becomes than
the irrational beasts when he plots against his fellow humans and
deprives them of the use of goods which he should be sharing
with them. A further point is that animals always have the awareness that they are merely using their grazing grounds and do not
regard them as a permanent possession. But humans very often
forget that everything is common to everyone, and indeed given
only for use and enjoyment; no one has a right to bring these
things under their own possession and ownership: "For everything has been made common to everyone to enjoy the use of
only—it is not to be anyone's private property."[82]

Exceptionally characteristic and graphic is what St Symeon
writes about those people who appropriate what is common,

80 See the contribution of Fr George Tsetsis in *Enemerosis* (vol. 3, 1985), the bulletin
    of the Permanent Representation of the Ecumenical Patriarchate to the World
    Council of Churches. Discussing this moral problem, Tsetsis also points to the sig-
    nificant role that local Churches can play, not only by putting forward as a model
    the patristic, ascetic use of the world and view of how the goods of the earth should
    be managed, but also by calling on governments to review their agricultural eco-
    nomic policy when such policies are proving detrimental to other human beings.
81 *Catechetical Orations* 9, SC 194, p. 110.
82 *Ibid.*, p. 112.

overcome by avarice, that is, insatiable consumerist greed. When avarice enters into people's lives, he says, is seems to operate just like a tyrant who makes tools and slaves and servants of the people themselves, and it shares out and apportions in various directions and ways what was given for common use and to all people by God, the Master and Creator of all. Once it has put fences and towers around these places which are common to all and locked them behind bars and gates, it deprives all the other people of their enjoyment of the Master's goods, while itself shamelessly pursuing mastery of everything and believing, furthermore, that it is not wronging anyone by doing so. In consequence, every one of the servants and slaves of this tyrant becomes successively, not a master and lord of the things and the wealth that has been laid up, but a wicked slave and a guard. If at some point such people are compelled to give a little or even all of their wealth to some of their hitherto despised brethren who are in need, they can by no means be regarded as merciful, or be credited with having fed Christ Himself,[83] or contributed some work worthy of reward. This is because they have acted from fear of punishment in hell or out of an expectation and hope that they would "receive a hundredfold," or have simply given in to the misfortune and miseries of their fellow men. So far from being able to justify themselves and be accounted merciful, they should know that they owe repentance until the end of their life because for years they had held goods from God's creation and withheld use of them from others of their brethren, who remained "in straitened circumstances and in want."[84]

Here it should be noted that it has always been the Church's teaching that the good things in the world have God as their sole

83 Cf. Mt 25:35.
84 *Catechetical Orations* 9, SC 104, p. 112. On abuse as a lack of social justice see also the study by I. Petrou, *Social Justice—The Problem of Social Justice in the Orthodox Tradition* (in Greek) (Thessaloniki, 1986), especially pp. 50-75; Archimandrite Nektarios Hadjimichalis (now Metropolitan of Leros and Kalymnos), *Views on Private Property in the Church during the First Three Centuries* (in Greek) (Thessaloniki, 1972).

owner and lord.[85] God offers them to all and not just to some, so that they can provide for the needs they encounter in their earthly life. No one has the right to appropriate God's goods. On the contrary, these things are offered for use by all people on an equal basis, since all are equal before God. Just as in God's eyes there are no superior or inferior people, nor are other distinctions or social differences recognized, so also in relation to the goods of creation everyone has the same rights of use. "The treasures are common, from the common storehouse of God's creations," says St Gregory Palamas.[86] St Symeon sees as supremely poor those who have "wealth put away," since no man has ever been able to take with him any of what he has gained in the present life.[87] Hence wealth is perhaps the most tragic form of abuse of the world, since it takes people's hope away from God and turns it towards the things given by Him to be used only in this life here.

As with every sin committed by man, however, the misuse of material goods does not mean at all that the original cause of the sin is matter *per se*, since the inventor of sin, the devil, sinned without any influence from the material element. The Fathers stress that man's enslavement to matter is an intolerable situation, because it presupposes stagnation in his spiritual life.[88] Matter on

---

85 Since these things come from God, they are all "very good" and cannot be divided into those to be rejected and those to be accepted. Hence they should all be received with thanksgiving. See St Basil, *Short Rules* 92, PG 31.1145C: "On this, the first thing to be said is that if any of our possessions were evil *per se*, it would not be God's creation. For 'everything created by God is good, and nothing is to be rejected.' Secondly, that the Lord's command taught us not to reject possessions as evil and avoid them, but to use them prudently. And if one is condemned, it is not for having things at all, but for having a wrong attitude to things or for not using them well."

86 Hom. 13, PG 151.164B. See idem, Homs. 3 and 8, PG 151.37D and 353C respectively. See also Clement of Alexandria, *The Instructor* 2,12, 120,5, PG 8.545B. On all this see I. Petrou, *op. cit.*, p.52.

87 *Hymns* 48, SC 196, p. 134.

88 St Maximus the Confessor says characteristically: "...since standing still in virtue is the beginning of evil, when the intellect is concerned in an impassioned way with the material things lying on either side of the path." *To Thalassius on Various Difficulties*, PG 90.304D.

its own cannot cause any evil. The static and retarded soul causes the body, too, to remain outside sanctification and to transmit to the soul its own sluggishness. This happens when the soul does not develop the powers of the intellect in a proper and integral way but is imprisoned in matter. Losing its agility, it then begins to resemble sluggish matter and does nothing except serve matter, without however being able to transfigure it and raise it up to the sphere of divine life, offering it eucharistically to God.[89]

The one-sided nourishment of man and the satisfaction of the body alone without giving corresponding nourishment to the soul constitutes for St Symeon another form of abuse of the material world. As he underlines characteristically, this is what happens: whereas we have such a generous and loving Master and God who gives us things surpassing "our understanding, our hearing and our thinking" just for having faith in Him, we disdain these things and prefer to be nourished only with earthly and material things, like the dumb animals. Yet these things too have been given by God's great compassion and providence for man "to satisfy the body's need," so that he may be nourished by them "in moderation" and not with excess and abuse. Thus the soul too is given the possibility of pursuing its course towards God without hindrance, being nourished by the food of the Holy Spirit, according to the measure of its purification from passions and its spiritual ascent.[90] Besides, as he observes elsewhere, if a man satiates his flesh by over-eating, it is not possible for his soul to enjoy the divine goodness at the same

89 See N. Matsoukas, *World, Man and Communion According to Maximus the Confessor* (in Greek), p. 77.

90 *Catechetical Orations* 22, SC 104, pp. 380-2: "...we have such a generous Master, so full of love for mankind that in return just for faith in Him He grants us such gifts as surpass our understanding, our hearing and our thinking... But we like dumb animals prefer earth alone, and the things that, through His great mercy, are produced by the earth to satisfy our bodily needs. These are given for us to be nourished in moderation, so that our soul may make its journey to the things above without hindrance, being likewise nourished with intelligible food, the food of the Spirit, to the extent that it is cleansed and ascends."

time. For it is obvious that the more one tries to satisfy one's gluttony, the more one deprives oneself of the divine sweetness. On the
other hand, according to the measure of one's struggle to bring into
subjection the desires of the flesh, one receives spiritual nourishment and the soul is filled with consolation and heavenly joy.[91]

When man persists in abusing the world, he ends up ascribing
autonomy to the capacities and potentialities which are innate to
him as gifts of God's love. While he tries to develop these to an
ever greater degree, they ultimately become exceptionally dangerous to his very survival, since the way in which he affirms these
capacities is part and parcel of the abuse. It is not unusual to find
that neither our hard work nor our technological or other
achievements are able to help us improve our life, because they
malfunction when tangled up in a general view of the world
which is purely one of utilitarianism and abuse. Not infrequently,
movements for justice, peace, and freedom also become
embroiled in the whirl and confusion of this abuse, when instead
of being possibilities for true communion with God and other
people, they are given autonomy as values and ends in themselves,
destined to operate within the nexus of self-seeking and in the service of suspect interests.

As has been stressed, however, man's knowledge and potentialities are "garments of skin" which are only a temporary and intermediate solution. When these too are made autonomous and seen
as containing their purpose within themselves, and when man
wants to live in these "garments" only—then this is the ultimate
delusion, the final self-imprisonment in corruption. From this
point of view, autonomous and arrogant humanism is nothing
but a naive exaltation and glorification of death. Abuse of the

91 *Chapters* 1.42, SC 51, p. 62: "It is impossible both to fill the flesh to satiety with
food, and to enjoy spiritually the immaterial and divine goodness. For the more one
serves the belly, the more one deprives oneself of that goodness. But insofar as one
mortifies the body, one will correspondingly be filled with spiritual nourishment
and consolation."

world has as its consequence "everything else that belongs to this transient life," i.e., vainglory, envy, quarrelling, deceit, grumbling and everything that is abhorrent in God's sight and endangers man's soul.[92]

Forms of abuse of the world are to be found today in what we call Western civilization. This automatically highlights the extent to which the view of the world and of man in the West has diverged from that of the Orthodox East. Despite the fact that scholastic thought accepted from Christian cosmology the truth about man as microcosm and the world as "*macroanthropos*," it nonetheless attempted to bring it down to the level of the cognitive powers of analogical reasoning; this means interpreting the relationship between microcosm and macrocosm within the framework of a rationalistic mode of thinking which makes the world into an object vis-à-vis the logic of a utilitarian epistemology.[93]

The chief upshot of this view is the anthropocentric world image of humanism, which tries to subordinate the truth of the world to man, and that in the context of an intellectual or mechanical domination. If we regard the admission of rationalism into Western theology not as an isolated phenomenon but as symptomatic of the whole way in which that theology was moving, then it is able to justify and explain perfectly the rejection by Western theologians of the distinction between the essence and energies of God (which was a feature mainly of the fourteenth century). It equally explains the rejection of any personal view of the inner principle of things in the world, which in the final analysis means denying the revelation of God's personal energy in creation.

92 *Catechetical Orations* 2, SC 96, p. 272.
93 See M.-D. Chenu, *La théologie comme science au XIIIe siècle* (Paris, 1969), pp. 97f., where the writer sees in the works of Thomas Aquinas an "outstanding" synthesis of the speculative character of theology with the demands of scientific rationality; idem, *La théologie au douzième siècle* (Paris, 1966), p. 49; E. Gilson, *La philosophie au moyen age* (Paris, 1962), p. 327. For a critical appraisal of this theology see Ch. Yannaras, *The Person and Eros* (in Greek) (Athens, 1976), pp. 133f.

This second rejection had a decisive effect on the practice of the West in the culture of the Renaissance. This culture lashed out in frenzy, trying to eliminate everything that did not agree with the logic and reason that renaissance man had imposed on nature. And it is well known that "reason" from the Renaissance onwards meant rationalism. So whatever did not accord with rationalism, i.e. with common sense and mathematics, was unacceptable to renaissance man,[94] while an approach of utilitarianism and domination was adopted in relation to nature and the environment. It would not be an exaggeration to observe that Gothic architecture is, historically at least, the first glaring example of the cultural and, more specifically, technological ramifications of the cosmology of the medieval theologians who promoted a peculiar anthropocentricity. For it is on this cosmology that the entire edifice of so-called Western or technological civilization is founded. Curious as the contention may seem, it is not arbitrary to relate the genesis of technocracy to theology, since the development of technical skill in the West is not just a phenomenon of rapid scientific progress, but at the same time the concrete expression of a particular *attitude* to the world: an attitude which sums up all stages of the religious development of Western man.[95]

Yet the abuse of creation, whatever form it may take, is not caused either by natural science or by technology *per se*. The scientific conclusions of modern physics could have been the starting point for understanding the world not as a deterministically organized mechanical (or rather, mechanistic) arrangement, but as a harmony of infinite and indeterminate differentiations of a supremely personal energy, which is the energy of God. This, however, presupposes that technology too will have respect for creation as its starting point, that it will be interested in

94 See A. Keselopoulos, "The Violation of Creation and the 'Alternative Solution,'" p. 501.

95 Ch. Yannaras, *op. cit.*, p. 144. See also P. Michelis, *An Aesthetic View of Byzantine Art* (in Greek) (Athens, 1972), pp. 89-90.

knowledge of things rather than in their use, while making the truth of the world rather than its utility the aim of its every task.[96]

If it is not practicable today to do away with technology, it is nevertheless practicable to reject its autonomous status, which expresses itself as technocracy. If it is not possible to eliminate technical knowledge from human life, it is possible to tame it and make it serve to improve the quality of that life. Man's attempt to subordinate the natural order to his individual needs—a subordination achieved through the power of the human mind actualized in the machine—is ultimately a failure, because it has proved not only a torment and corruption of nature, but also an inescapable torment and a mortal threat to man himself: and hence a use of technology "in accordance with nature" must aim to bring man's life into harmony with the life of the world around him. Any attempt to improve the conditions of human life which violates such a harmony—such as the building of cities with all modern amenities in regions which are virtually desert—is doomed to failure in the long term.

The violation and abuse of creation frequently wears the mask of an excessive worship of that creation—or rather, of our own idea of what creation should be. Thus we build luxury hotels on unspoilt beaches, and houses or whole developments in beauty spots. We love being surrounded with greenery, and therefore insist on lawns and gardens however dry the climate and however

96 Characteristic and exceptionally revealing is S. Kyriazopoulos' discussion of man's sovereignty over the world, as well as of the abuse of the world by human need and desire, actualized by technology, in his book *The Origin of the Technical Spirit* (in Greek) (Athens, 1965), pp. 275-6: "What is required by technology is not knowledge, but *use*. The purpose of the mechanical task is not truth, but *utility*. Our age in concerned, not with what nature is, but with what can be *produced* through nature. The technical attitude, then, does not characterize only those uninvolved in scientific research; it also characterizes natural science, since research is advanced only by technical means. Instead, therefore, of technology being presented as applied science, natural science is presented as a methodical development of the technical mentality. This mentality is orientated not towards contemplation, but through contemplation to *power*."

limited the local water supply. But this is an instance of worshipping the creation "rather than the Creator"—which, as we have seen, St Symeon points to as the nadir of its defilement: "All creation, deified now and worshipped by man, is soiled and brought down to complete corruption."[97] Thus for today's technological civilization, characterized not by relationship with or use of the things of the world but by their consumption and misuse, it seems that escaping from the dead end of all the forms of abuse that it creates is more a spiritual matter than a scientific one—however much ecologists and environmentalists may fail to see this. Orthodox theology does not give recipes for a piecemeal approach to each problem as it arises, but it does offer a framework for a definitive way out of the tangled web they create. This will be the subject of the chapters which follow.

---

97 *Ethical Discourses* 1.2, SC 122, p. 194; *On the Mystical Life*, vol. 1, p. 30, where he also says: "Nothing else so soils the work of God and makes unclean what is clean as the deification of creation, and the worshipping of it as equal to God the Creator and Maker."

4

Right Use of the World

1. The inner principles of existent things

We saw in the first chapter that the world is the result of God's energies and a manifestation of His creative inner principle or "Word" (of the person of God the Word) through essences different in kind from the essence of God. The material reality of the world and the infinity of forms-substances that give shape to this reality are a result of the free personal and creative energy of God. This creative energy of God effected the purpose which He gave to matter, set the world in motion, and operates through the natural laws, with which the world was already developing before the appearance of man. Hence the natural laws too reflect in a certain way the wisdom of God, which is why there is such objective rationality in the world. Thus while the world remains in its essence different from God, it is at the same time a "word" which reveals the personal and creative uniqueness of God.

The personal mode of man's relationship with the world is called in the language of the Fathers "natural contemplation." This is the stage of spiritual life which comes between *action* and *theology*. St Maximus the Confessor regards "natural contemplation" as "being the mid-point between types and truth."[1] The aim of natural contemplation, then, is the study of God's "word" in nature and the discovery of His personal and creative uniqueness through the beauty, artistry, and wisdom that exist in things. According to Gregory of Nyssa, "the wisdom contemplated in creation is a word, albeit not

1   *On Various Questions*, PG 90.752A.

articulated."[2] For man, this is the personal "word" of the world, the first empirical confirmation of the presence of the personal God-the-Word—which is not to say, of course, that it is a manifestation of His person.[3] If creation has the potentiality, according to the favorite expression of St Basil, even "in silence" to "proclaim its Creator and Lord,"[4] this is due to the fact that when the creative energies of God were first manifested, the inner principles in accordance with which things were created and are organized were laid down and formulated at the same time. For this reason, the deeper man goes into the inner principles of existent things, the more he sees the greatness and more generally the energies of God and is led to His glory.[5] At the same time he realizes that the strong bond between created and uncreated nature is manifested and attested by the indissoluble relationship existing between the inner principles of things and the creative will of God in Trinity.

Knowledge of the inner principles that exist in created things leads to knowledge of the divine will, since matter for Orthodox cosmology is not just a reality which simply has its cause and first principle in God, but a substantiation of God's will and a result of the personal divine energy. It is a "word" which manifests the divine energy. As St Gregory of Nyssa very pertinently remarks, created things were not rearranged into their present form out of some existing matter, but the very divine will itself became the matter and essence of created things;[6] this means that the divine

---

2   *Hexaemeron*, PG 44.73C; see also 73A: "we should believe that in every existent thing there is a certain inner principle (or "word"), wise and full of artistry, even though it may surpass our vision."

3   Maximus the Confessor, *Theological Chapters* 3, PG 90.1261D: "Understanding the spiritual inner principles of visible things, man is taught that there is a creator of sensible things, while the question of what this creator is like he leaves uninvestigated, as being beyond him. For the visible creation clearly affords an understanding of the fact that there is a Creator, but not what the creator is like."

4   *On the Beginning of Proverbs*, 3, PG 31.392B.

5   Basil, *op. cit.*, PG 31.392AB. See also *idem*, *On Psalm* 33, 3, PG 29.357AB.

6   *Hom. on 1 Corinthians 15*, 28, PG 44.1312A.

will, as the logical cause and composition of created reality, is to be found materialized in the inner principle of each being. And since matter constitutes the substantiation of the divine will, the inner principles of matter, in other words its different forms and shapes, reflect the creative principles of the divine intentions and acts of will.[7] Thus the inner principles of existent things also become for man a source of the divine will.

The inner principles of existent things, or the "good wills," as they are called by saints of God, were prepared and planned by the will of the trinitarian God before the creation of the ages and the world. These principles are invisible and integral within the uncreated God Himself, Who made creation out of non-being in accordance with them.[8] All God's creations have as their foundation and inner constitution the principles of God, which are manifested through these things He has made: the inner principles of existent things are "seen, being understood from the things made," because when man approaches created things "in accordance with nature" and with the "proper science," they all announce and proclaim the principles/reasons for which they were created.[9] Hence the existence of rationality in the created world leads us to the supra-rational person of the Word, who is the source of reason and of every reality. So as man partakes of material creation and eats food to satisfy his body, at the same time he nourishes his spirit, not only with the rationality of the world but also with the inner principles of divine love, with the divine Word who loves man and is the bread of eternal life, according to St Maximus.[10]

7 See *idem, Hexaemeron*, PG 44.73C: "... by a certain word the power producing each of the things that come into being is brought into action."

8 "The inner principles of things [were] prepared beforehand by the God of the ages as He knows, and are invisible; it is the habit of godly men to call them also 'good wills'." Maximus the Confessor, *To Thalassius*, PG 90.293D-296A, and *On Various Difficulties*, PG 91.1080A.

9 *To Thalassius,* PG 90.296A.

10 *On the Lord's Prayer*, PG 90.871ff. Cf. D. Staniloae, "The World as Gift and Sacrament of God's Love," p. 667.

In every detail of creation and over the whole range of things in it, from elementary matter to the highest forms of life, creation has in its composition and structure a rationality, an inner principle or reason. In other words, it is not only the reason or principle of personal beings that is assigned by God. Non-rational creation, despite being thought of as an impersonal reality, has its order and arrangement from the Creator, and hence it possesses a rationality and exhibits a rational composition in its structure, because it is God who unites sensible and intelligible beings. *Logos*, this "reason" or "principle," is always a uniting element, while irrationality is divisive: "For *logos* is the union of things divided; irrationality (*alogia*) is the division of things united," as St Maximus characteristically states.[11]

St Symeon the New Theologian refers in many of his writings to the inner principles of the entities in creation, and he underlines the importance for man of discovering and understanding them. In particular, he stresses that man is led to an increase in faith and upward progress in love for God through varied and divers signs, among which is the "contemplation of the inner principles of creation."[12] For one cannot acquire perfect love for God as an inalienable possession without spiritual knowledge of the principle of created things,[13] through which God, their Creator and Maker, is contemplated.

Through the inner principle of created things we have the harmony of the world in action, which constitutes the potentiality

11   *On the Lord's Prayer*, PG 90.877BC; see also N. Matsoukas, *World, Man and Communion*, pp. 82-92, for a more detailed examination of the meaning of the inner principles of things in patristic thought.

12   *Theological Discourses* 1, SC 122, p. 110: "Believers receive this [the teaching of faith] through varied and divers signs; through riddles, through mirrors, through mystical and ineffable energies, through divine revelations, though dim illuminations, through contemplation of the inner principles of creation, and many other things through which daily their faith increases and they progress upward to love of God."

13   *Chapters* 1.33, SC 51, p. 58. Cf. Wis 13:5, "For by the greatness and beauty of the creatures, proportionably the Maker of them is seen"; cf. Rom 1:20.

for man's personal relationship with the world, and also a potentiality for his personal relationship with the Maker. This is why the purpose of things and also of man—in other words the *logos* of their existence, their *raison d'être*—is a fundamental element in the theology of St Symeon the New Theologian. Understanding and seeing the purpose of one's existence takes precedence over any other participation in and experience of the reality of creation.[14] Furthermore, as he notes elsewhere, this constitutes man's salvation—his remaining safe and whole.[15]

In contrast with the irrationality that produces division, the inner principles of things are always the unitive element which connects God's animate creation with His inanimate creation. The right relationship between man and the rest of creation requires the personal discovery of the inner principle of each thing, and at the same time leads to a eucharistic use of it.[16] Such a relationship, however, means that man has in practice abandoned the tendency to subordinate everything and respects what surrounds him, because he is convinced that things in creation are not impersonal objects of use, but works and creations, the results of action and creation by a personal God. The uniqueness of the inner principle of each thing constitutes the personal character of the data of the world.

As man breathes the air that is in creation or enjoys the good things produced in creation, he has the possibility of apprehending the inner principles of things and the existence of reciprocal relationships between them; at the same time, he himself grows and is spiritually enriched by this experience.[17] But perfect knowledge of the inner principles of existent things, according to St Symeon the New Theologian, is associated principally with that

14 *Catechetical Orations* 2, SC 96, p. 242: "... do not give sleep to your eyes nor delight your throat with the pleasure of food, until you see how and for what purpose you were called, and what you are hastening to attain as your goal."

15 *Chapters* 3.67, SC 51, p. 160.

16 *Catechetical Orations* 5, SC 96, pp. 388-390.

17 Cf. Staniloae, "The World as Gift and Sacrament," p. 663.

state in which man has acquired experience of the baptism of tears—of repentance as a path and way of life. For our first baptism "has the water that foreshadows tears, and the chrism that signifies beforehand the intelligible chrism of the Spirit."

If the first baptism is a type of the truth, then the second, the baptism of tears, is the very truth itself,[18] which reveals the inner principles of things to man as manifestations of God's will and directs him to a true relationship with Him and with His creation.

The existence of the world in itself does not guarantee man a true perception of the nature of existent things and in consequence a genuine encounter with the inner principles of the things in creation. Enslavement to the passions is always a hindrance to this encounter. Man needs first of all to make himself receptive to the baptism of tears in order to experience true repentance as a change in his way of thinking, so that he may then be given the possibility of orientating himself properly relative to creation and developing a relationship of love with the things of the world. Just as at night, says St Symeon, we are able to see with our physical eyes only in that place where we have lit a lamp, while all the rest of the world is in night and darkness to our eyes; in the same way for those who are in the night and darkness of sin and content with it, our good Master and Lord Christ, bearing in mind human infirmity and weakness, becomes the lamp which lightens our spiritual darkness, despite the fact that He is God and remains uncontainable for all. Then, suddenly, man raises his eyes and "looks upon the nature of existent things" in a way such as he had never known before; he feels amazement and wonder, while tears come to him of their own accord although he feels no pain, and by them his mind is purified and baptized into the second baptism.[19]

The inner principles or "words" of existent things have their source, their substance, and their end in God the Word. It is from

18 *Chapters* 1.36, SC 51, p. 60.
19 *Chapters* 1.35, SC 51, pp. 58-60.

these principles that the objective rationality of the world flows. Thus the world reflects and "tells" the glory of God.[20] Precisely for this reason, St Symeon insists that man needs to have the awareness of the image of the God-man Jesus Christ, with the help of the rational and intellective[21] part of his soul, in order to be able to know and encounter the inner principle of things. Otherwise, he remains flesh and blood, unable to acquire through the "word" of things alone an "awareness of spiritual glory," just as people blind from birth are unable to see and know the light of the sun even though someone might describe it to them in words.[22]

The need for a spiritual perception of the world and of things is stressed very frequently in St Symeon's writings, since no one can discover and encounter the inner principles of materials creations with their physical eyes alone: "The height of heaven and the breadth of the earth and the proportions (*logoi*) of everything else are things that no one can understand properly using their physical eyes alone."[23] Besides, how can things that transcend the human intellect and mind be comprehended with bodily eyes? But once man's intellect is cleansed of troublesome reasonings, freed from prepossessions and enlightened by the mercy and grace of God, then according to the measure of this enlightenment he will be able to see and observe *the contemplation of existent* things.[24]

This is why the Church, recognizing that man even in his state of spiritual darkness is still an image of God, albeit an obscured

20 "The heavens are telling the glory of God; and the firmament proclaims His handiwork," Ps 18:1.

21 Translator's note: i.e. that associated with the *nous*, or spiritual intellect, the faculty capable of direct apprehension of spiritual realities.

22 *Chapters* 1.53, SC 51, p. 68: "One who has not knowingly and with clear awareness put on the image of our Lord Jesus Christ, the heavenly man and God, in the rational and intelligible man—this person is still only flesh and blood, unable to receive an awareness of spiritual glory through the 'word' of things, just as those born blind are not able to know the light of the sun through words alone." Cf. 1 Cor 15:49-50.

23 *Chapters* 1.34, SC 51, p. 58.

24 *Ibid.*

one, and preserves the embers of divine truth, attempts to "make man word" (or "make him rational") and lead him ultimately to deification. Thus she affirms man's searching and research in the world, because she believes that this is invisibly directed by God's love, and that in consequence he is doing nothing other than "feeling after" the true God,[25] even if the Fall and spiritual darkness do not allow man to recognize Him. The human being seeks Christ as the inner principle, the "word" of the world, without really knowing it, because he is created in the image of Christ the Word.[26]

2. Use of the world in accordance with nature

An approach to the inner principles of existent things (i.e. knowing God's inner principles according to which the world was made) requires that we use the world "in accordance with nature" and look at it "with the proper science."[27] According to Orthodox theology, there is unity between man and creation only when creation is used in accordance with nature. Only such a use guarantees that the inner principles which the Maker has placed in things are saved and preserved. This is not only a commandment of God, but also an essential precondition for preserving the balance of nature itself. In Deuteronomy[28] God orders the protection of trees, while further on it is underlined that one of the main reasons for keeping the sabbath is that the animals need to rest. Man is the steward and guard of the garden of Eden, i.e. of the prototypical biblical image of

25 Cf. Acts 17:27, "...that they might feel after Him and find Him."

26 Cf. Protopresbyter Georgios Metallinos, "Ecological Correspondences and Differences between Hellenism and Christianity—Their Attitude to the Environment" (in Greek), in *Koinonia* (Athens, 1985), vol. 4, p. 506.

27 Maximus the Confessor, *To Thalassius*, PG 90.296A: "For all the works God has made, when contemplated by us wisely, in accordance with nature and with the proper science, mysteriously proclaim to us the principles according to which they were made."

28 20:19-20.

nature before it revolted.[29] He is in an indissoluble relationship with the animals and plants. He gives names, and this action permanently links Creator, man, and created things.[30]

The unity of the universe and life that is in accordance with nature is devoid of irrationality. Here reason prevails, which is the union of things divided.[31] Any disruption in relations between man and the environment is an indication that irrationality has infiltrated these relations. According to the Fathers, irrationality and unnaturalness at all levels of relationships and of life constitute the state of passions, which gives rise to fragmentation and division. In contrast with the passions, which express themselves in "immoderation," "abuse," and what is contrary to nature, the truly virtuous life exhibits a use of all God's creations which is "moderate" and in accordance with nature.[32]

This view of spiritual life can be seen in the teaching of St Symeon the New Theologian too. The struggle to preserve the image in man is identified with remaining within the limits of nature, with "behaving in accordance with nature."[33] More specifically, referring to the relation between man and the world, he presents remaining within the limits of nature as a precondition for offering creation up in praise and being led from the beauty of created things to the author of existence and maker of all.[34] Living as he does in God's creation, man's attitude should be that of one

29 Gen 2:15.
30 Cf. N. Nissiotis, "Nature as Creation," p. 15.
31 Cf. Maximus the Confessor, *On the Lord's Prayer,* PG 90.877BC.
32 See A. Keselopoulos, *Passions and Virtues,* pp. 23ff.
33 "Behaving according to nature is an inviolable guard of the image and the dignity from above," *Chapters* 1.65, SC 51, p. 76.
34 *Theological Discourses* 2, SC 122, p. 145: "For one who believes that God is the maker of all and that He brought forth all things out of nothing, in heaven and on earth and under the earth—being himself created by God, such a one remains within his own limits, knowing his maker. And being drawn by the beauty of created things to the author of existence Himself, he praises and glorifies Him as Creator of all..."

who "has already received what is natural, and no longer looks upon the creatures of God in a manner which is unnatural."[35] For a use of the world which denies the inner principle of creation and the natural state does not only abuse creation, but torments man himself as well. It subjugates the world—which is regarded and used as an impersonal object—destroying and violating the inner principle of things in order ultimately to serve man's "needs" and greed according to utilitarian criteria. In this way, however, it alienates man as well, anaesthetizing, harassing, and mortifying him. Many "who are contrary to nature are outside everything," and, even though they have eyes, they are unable to see and understand the wonders of God's creation; they are in the world as dead men even before their death.[36]

The use of inanimate creation in accordance with nature, however, requires first and foremost an attitude to animate creation which is in accordance with nature—one of respect and love. St Symeon stresses that Christians should look upon all people with the same love as they would Christ Himself. They should be ready to give even their life for them.[37] They should not regard anyone as evil, but see all people as good. Even when they perceive that some brother is being tempted by the devil and troubled by passions, they should hate the passions and not the brother who is assailed by them. If they see someone being harried and tormented by evil desires and prepossessions, they should show extra compassion and sympathy since, given the mutability of human nature, they could easily find themselves subject to the same temptation some time.[38]

This counsel of our holy Father has a basis in ecclesiology. Wanting to stress the relation between the common and the

---

35 *Ethical Discourses* 6, SC 129, p. 154; *On the Mystical Life,* vol. 2, p. 79.
36 *Hymns* 32, SC 174, p. 402.
37 Cf. Jn 15:13.
38 *Chapters* 3.3, SC 51, pp. 120-2.

particular as it applies to the one human nature and the many human persons, he underlines that the variety and the differences in gifts among the members of the body of Christ are due to the fact that the manifestation of the Holy Spirit is given to each believer in proportion to his receptivity and also his own spiritual interests. Furthermore, the Holy Spirit distributes and activates all the gifts in each person as He wishes.[39] Just as each believer receives the place appointed to him in God's "mansions"[40] according to his worth, so also within the body of the Church each person is reckoned and "numbered" as a member of Christ according to the measure that he is worthy of it.[41]

At this point we must stress the difference between virtue, and gift or charism. Virtue is achieved through man's care, effort, and struggle, while charisms are bestowed on man as gifts of God.[42] Hence the person who leaves undeveloped the gifts he has received from God bears a great responsibility. St Symeon has one catechetical discourse entitled "That it is not without danger to bury the talent given us by God; for it is necessary to publicize this talent and show it to everyone and gratefully proclaim God's benefactions for the good of those who hear it, even though some may be displeased;"[43] here he talks about making available the talents which each person has received as a way of offering them back to God through the communion of persons, and as a way of working and co-creating in the world which God has created and maintains.

Again, the disharmony to be seen in creation is due to man's refusal to cultivate the gifts—the talents—that God has given

39 *Ethical Discourses* 1.6, SC 122, p. 230; *On the Mystical Life,* vol. 1, p. 46. See also 1 Cor 12:11-14.

40 Jn 14:2.

41 *Ethical Discourses* 1.6, SC 122, p. 230; *On the Mystical Life,* vol. 1, p. 46. A more detailed and systematic formulation of these ideas is to be found in Nikitas Stethatos' *Treatise on Hierarchy,* SC 81, pp. 293ff.

42 *Catechetical Orations* 18, SC 104, pp. 294-6, where examples are also given.

43 *Catechetical Orations* 34, SC 113, pp. 270-302.

him, and thus to serve creation. When man refuses to be a creative presence—to "till and keep" creation—and remains in the laziness and sloth engendered by his egotistic estrangement from God, he becomes a "useless instrument" "because he has not been willing to carry out the commandments of the Creator."[44] Further, this refusal of communion and co-operation with God does not only render man himself "useless," but also leads him to abuse and prostitute nature; and then he is a danger to the rest of creation too, since he becomes "the instrument of every wickedness, an accomplished tool of every lawlessness and evil work."[45]

Here it should be underlined that man's refusal to serve the world in the proper way and to cultivate the gifts given him by God does not leave him simply in an neutral state, but leads him into a state contrary to nature, which is that of passions and sin. Other Fathers too, such as St Gregory Palamas, see immoderation and abuse of the good things of God's creation as root causes of the passions.[46] A satisfaction of desires which is foreign to the measure of nature alienates man and leads him from what is in accordance with nature to what is contrary to it. Food, for example, is a God-given good and a necessity for man; but misuse of it creates the passions of gluttony, excessive drinking and drunkenness, while at the same time exciting the sexual passions. This is why in another instance the same Father stresses that man's love contrary to nature for created things or even for his own body is the root of "evil passions and the whole host of sins."[47] When, on the other hand, man remains within the limits of what is in accordance with nature, then as St Symeon says he becomes not only a

44 *Hymns* 54, SC 196, p. 242.

45 *Ibid.*, p. 244.

46 *In Defence of the Holy Hesychasts* 2.2.19; *Works of Gregory Palamas*, ed. P. Chrestou, vol. 1 (Thessaloniki, 1962), p. 527.

47 Hom. 33, PG 151.417CD. On the meaning of "contrary to nature" and empassioned use of the world, see A. Keselopoulos, *Passions and Virtues* p. 24ff.

son of the Most High and god by grace, but also a "useful tool working all good."[48]

The spiritual struggle, the keeping of the divine commandments, and indeed every kind of work by which people make a living, are to be understood simply as a thanksgiving and an offering of praise to God for all the good things He has given us.[49] Then work becomes a eucharistic service to the God and Creator of all, and also to other people. Thus no work, however arduous, can be regarded by the Christian as demeaning, since it is still an opportunity for expressing thanks to God.[50] The harmony of creation is complemented by the diversity of human gifts and tasks of service. Referring to some particular tasks or trades, such as that of the sailor, the farmer, the agronomist, the soldier etc., St Symeon talks about the particularity of the human person, which is lived out through each occupation and which has been given by God Himself.[51] Furthermore, the way in which the different occupations complement each other to provide for the bodily needs of human nature is taken up by our holy Father and applied to matters of spiritual life as well. Human life, he observes, is made up of different crafts and sciences, in which each person works and contributes his services to the communal whole from some special skill and where all people live in a community, sometimes offering their service to others and at other times partaking of others' services. This is precisely what should happen in spiritual matters too. One person may have one virtue highly developed in his life and may practise that, while another follows a different path; but all should be running towards the same goal.[52]

48 *Hymns* 54, SC 196, p. 248.
49 *Catechetical Orations* 5, SC 96, p. 452.
50 *Catechetical Orations* 5, SC 96, pp. 454-6.
51 "Hence each is fitted for a craft—not the one he wants himself,
    but the one for which he was created,
    and to this he is disposed properly and by nature.
    For behold, the craftsman Word fashioned me
    such as He wished, and placed me in the world." (*Hymns* 54, SC 196, pp. 240-2)
52 *Chapters* 3.66, SC 51, p. 160.

All God's creations are good in their nature and essence, and remain so. The use of creations and of the world by man may be good or evil. Furthermore, man himself does not change his nature when he moves into a state contrary to nature, a state of passions and abuse of God's creations. Formed good by God—who did not create anything evil—he remains unchanged in his nature and essence. What is changed and altered is man's voluntary choice and will. On man's good or evil choice and his use of the things of the world in accordance with nature or contrary to it depends the goodness or depravity of his works. For as the nature of a knife does not change whether it is put to use for good or evil, but it always remains iron, so also man acts and does what he wants, without either departing from his own nature or changing the nature of things. Any change or alteration relates to their use.[53] The world may become a negative influence on man's life, but this is due not to the world but to man's attitude to it. In this case, the word "world" is identified with that realm which is under the influence of the devil, while by contrast man in his openness and relationship with Christ acquires the possibility of escaping "from the depths of ignorance and the gloom of love for the world," which is influenced by demonic forces.[54]

Hence in matter there is nothing evil: there is only a healthy and an unhealthy attitude to it. So whereas matter used in accordance with nature coexists harmoniously with man, in the case where it is misused it "revolts" against him and alienates his life.[55] This is the reason why Orthodox cosmology promotes a use of the world that accords with nature and professes the unity of man with his fellow men and with the entire creation. This unity receives a mortal blow and may even be destroyed when our modern technological and urban culture offers man the goods of the earth through various consumer centers, thus alienating him

53 *Chapters* 3.90, SC 51, p. 178.
54 *Ethical Discourses* 4, SC 129, p. 20; *On the Mystical Life,* vol. 2, p. 17; cf. Jn 2:1ff.
55 *Catechetical Orations* 25, SC 113, p. 60.

irrevocably from his natural environment and presenting him with the offspring and nurslings of Creation as consumer goods, cut off from his personal life. For this reason, man in our society in particular has difficulty loving and respecting nature, whereas it is easy for him to exploit, pollute, and destroy it.

This does not, of course, mean that we must reject technology, but rather that we must require it to take its place within a life in accordance with nature and be of true service to man. For this to happen, however, the starting point for tackling the problem must be the composite anthropology of Orthodoxy, and not the choice of some sort of anthropological nestorianism or monophysitism.[56] It is very characteristic that this unity of spirit and matter in man is a hallmark of the whole of patristic theology and of the Orthodox tradition. Already in the second century, St Irenaeus of Lyons formulated the now classic anthropological principle on this subject when he said that "It is not a soul on its own or a body on its own, but the two together that are and are called man,"[57] while in the fourteenth century St Gregory Palamas will underline that "the spiritual man is made up of three things: the grace of the heavenly Spirit, a rational soul and an earthen body."[58] Since man is body, then, he participates in the physical world around him. Through man's senses, this world expresses itself and becomes perceptible. But because man is also spirit, he has an affinity with God in Trinity and a possibility of relating to Him. If technology does not ignore this reality, it is able to shape and give form to matter without the latter losing its inner principle; matter remains articulate. Only in this way will the horizon of our civilization really be broadened, and technology and economics will discover higher aspirations since the development of our world will be able to recognize its true orientation and discover the right

---

56 Translator's note: Christological heresies which compromise the full reality of Christ's divine nature (nestorianism) or his human nature (monophysitism).

57 *Against Heresies* 5.6.1, PG 7.1137A.

58 *In Defence of the Holy Hesychasts* 1.3.43; *Works of Gregory Palamas*, ed. P. Chrestou, vol. 1 (Thessaloniki, 1962), p. 454.

path—one that does not have built-in blind alleys—which leads
to its supreme goal in infinity.

As we have noted already, this was how Byzantine art func-
tioned—especially that art directly related to the worship of God.
Through hymnody or building or mosaic, matter is given a voice;
preserving the inner principle of its creation, it takes part in the
divine doxology. In Byzantine art everything remains within the
limits of what is in accordance with nature and of rational—
"*logos-ful*"—use, and becomes articulate, because it is made part
of a rhythm. Here all things preserve the unity of spirit and
matter, standing as reverberations of the harmony of the world of
the spirit within the world of matter. Hence the great importance
of mathematics in Byzantine aesthetics.[59]

It would be enough to study the architecture of just one
Byzantine building or the technique of stonework and the way
the stones are joined, in order to touch what is truly natural in the
relations between man and matter and to wonder at the ethos of
that culture. In Byzantine art, man respects and studies the inner
principle of the material, and does not force matter in order to
bring it into obedience to a purpose conceived by his own brain.
In his use of the materials of the world, he schools himself in
self-abnegation and a self-denial of egocentric vainglory and
brings out the possibilities which matter itself possesses to be
"made word" and to establish a dialogue with the craftsman such
as no rationalistic technique is able to duplicate. Hence, while the
idols of the gentiles are "silver and gold, the work of men's hands"
(Ps 134:15), our church buildings, the sacred vessels, the icons and
all the other monuments of Byzantine art can be called "not made
with hands," "wrought and built by God." For even though they
were constructed by human hands and with materials from the

---

59 See Gervase Mathew, *Byzantine Aesthetics* (London, 1964), p. 23, and A. Keselopoulos,
    "The Violation of Nature and the 'Alternative Solution,'" p. 502. [Translator's note: It
    is significant here that *logos* can equally mean "ratio."]

earth, they are holy and sacred. Thus "their construction is not a human device but a spiritual liturgy, a work of the Holy Spirit." They are "things performed by the divine energy through the energy (operation) of the flesh."[60]

A characteristic example is Hagia Sophia in Constantinople, where man as God's co-creator has made "most dear" matter transparent to the light of the transfiguration, free from the darkness of the demonic powers which monopolize it in the fallen world. There we see the disappearance of the weight, the meanness and also the luxury that the individual ego requires as its props, and the exaltation of matter to true grandeur and boundless fullness, a foreshadowing of its final transfiguration. For this reason, this art can very easily be distinguished even from today's "traditional" houses, which merely retain certain external features of the traditional architecture while being unable to connect these features with modern reality and while functioning for the most part in a way that wastes materials and violates nature.[61]

St Symeon the New Theologian lived historically within this cultural context that does not isolate any form of life into watertight compartments, and where spiritual and ecclesial life gives meaning and sustenance to the whole of human life. This is why he underlines so categorically that seeing the world in accordance with nature requires the performance of the divine commandments,

60 Archimandrite Vasileios of Iviron, *Theological Commentary on the Frescoes of the Holy Monastery of Stavronikita* (in Greek) (Reprinted from *The Cretan Painter Theophanes*, Holy Monastery of Stavronikita, [Athens: Domos, 1987], pp. 18-19).

61 On this subject see further J. Hussey, *Church and Learning in the Byzantine Empire* (London, 1937); P. Charanis, "On the Social Structure of the Later Roman Empire," *Byzantion* 17 (1944-45), pp. 38-57; M. Kalligas, *The Aesthetics of Space in the Greek Church in the Middle Ages* (in Greek) (Athens, 1946); Gervase Mathew, *Byzantine Aesthetics* (London: John Murray, 1964); F. Dvornik, *Early Christian and Byzantine Political Philosophy* (Dumbarton Oaks, 1966); A. Toynbee, *Constantine Porphyrogenitus and his World* (Oxford University Press); P. Michelis, *An Aesthetic View of Byzantine Art* (in Greek; 2nd ed., Athens, 1972), esp. pp. 85-98; Ch. Yannaras, *Elements of Faith: An Introduction to Orthodox Theology* (ET K. Schram, T. & T. Clarke, 1991), Ch. 6, "The World."

and is achieved by the enlightenment of the Holy Spirit.[62] Thus man acquires spiritual experience and a spiritual awareness of things that is the "one thing" and also the only thing that matters in his life. With this sense he is able to see all things clearly and rightly, while without it he is like a blind man. And "he who is blind to the one thing is altogether blind to everything, while he who sees in the one thing is in a position to contemplate all things. He enters into contemplation of all things and is outside what he contemplates; being in the one thing, such a person sees everything."[63] But this state is achieved by people who are spiritually far advanced, is accompanied by rapture of the senses to things above sense, and presupposes purification of the senses.[64] In this state, man ceases to look upon his environment with indifference, with an inclination to misuse it or even with superficial, external criteria. In contrast, he looks upon it with boundless respect because it is a work of God and feels an intense responsibility and love for it, such that he cannot bear any injury to it without being deeply pained. This is the relationship of man and environment in accordance with nature that the Fathers and teachers of the spiritual life enjoin. Thus when Abba Isaac the Syrian was asked "What is a merciful heart?" he replied with these amazing words: "It is a heart that burns for the entire creation, for humans, for birds, for animals, for the demons and for all created things. At the recollection and the sight of them, tears fall from such a person's eyes. From the great and intense love that constrains his heart he cannot bear to hear of or see any injury or any slight sorrow occurring in creation. At every moment he prays with tears for the dumb beasts and for the enemies of truth and for those who harm him and for the reptiles, that God will preserve them and have mercy on them."[65]

---

62 *Chapters* 1.4, SC 51, p. 42.

63 *Chapters* 1.51, SC 51, p. 68.

64 *Ethical Discourses* 3, SC 122, p. 408.

65 Ch. Spanos, ed., Hom. 81; *The Ascetic Homilies of St Isaac the Syrian*; translated by Holy Transfiguration Monastery (Boston, 1984), Hom. 71, pp. 344-5.

3. The ascetic—non-consumerist use of the world

It is particularly characteristic that St Symeon, the Church's mystical theologian par excellence, does not restrict the possibility of participation in the Kingdom of God to life after death only, but maintains that it is attainable and begins from this world and the present life, where it is manifested as, and identified with, the Christian's complete obedience to the will of God. In this case, he says, human beings are like the angels, bearing in their souls even in this life "God who is above all."[66] Besides, none of God's creations or the material goods which He provides for man is reprehensible or abhorrent; on the contrary, when used "as appropriate for the sustenance of the body" they are essential for human survival. Hence the proper attitude towards all material goods remains a reasoned use of the them, and at the same time avoidance of the "desire of the flesh," the "desire of the eyes," and the "vain boasting of the thoughts," which can so easily become part of man's life. If there is something that wounds man and does him mortal harm, that is sin and not the use of material things per se.[67]

An unproductive rejection and avoidance of the material goods of the world on the part of the Christian is not sufficient either to lead him to true dispassion, or to ensure him participation in the Kingdom of God. It is particularly significant that St Symeon the New Theologian—who belongs among the "neptic" and ascetic Fathers of the Church—stresses this fact. In this way, he gives us the proper way of looking at the subject, while on the other hand underlining the true dimensions of Orthodox spiritual life and its positive, dynamic character. It is one thing, he emphasizes, not to desire any of the "delightful" and "sweet"

---

66 *Ethical Discourses* 3, SC 122, p. 436; *On the Mystical Life,* vol. 1, p. 138: "So, too, do human beings become like cherubim in this world, bearing aloft on the backs of their souls Him who is God above all."

67 *Catechetical Orations* 5, SC 96, pp. 440-2.

things of this world, and quite another to desire and yearn for eternal and heavenly good things. The first state on its own cannot be taken as progress in the spiritual life, since many people for various reasons have looked on material goods with disdain, without correspondingly cultivating genuine spiritual life and showing true holiness. By contrast, the longing for eternal and heavenly good things is engendered only in the few who have put all the power of their souls into acquiring them.[68] Only in this case is abstention from material goods justified, because it is done for the love of God and understood as going beyond these things, not despising them. Again, fasting has never been regarded in the Orthodox Church as contempt for the "sinfulness" of material goods, but as a means in the spiritual struggle of the Christian, who in contrition and repentance considers himself unworthy even of this participation in the good things of God's creation.[69]

Yet the senses, with which man comes into contact with God's creations, often express his unreasonable desires, when he exists only as a biological individual and makes pleasure an end in itself in his life. Thus the hedonistic demands of the senses inform man about creation in a way that does not correspond to the truth of created things, since they alter the beauty of creation and oblige it to submit itself to the service of human individuality and gluttony. In this state, the senses do not know the true beauty of creation but only its distorted image, which, in subjection to man's unreasonable demands, ends up being a "fantasy" of the true and original beauty which God bestowed on His creations. Very characteristic is what St Isaac the Syrian says about this case: "Contemplation of created things,

68 *Ethical Discourses* 4, SC 129, pp. 12-14. St Symeon even goes so far as to distinguish between the dispassion of the soul and that of the body: "Dispassion of the soul is one thing, and that of the body is another. For the one sanctifies the body by its own radiance and the light of the Spirit, while the other of itself can be of no benefit to the person who possesses it," *Chapters* 1.86, SC 51, p. 92.

69 *Catechetical Orations* 12, SC 104, p. 174.

though pleasant, is a shadow of knowledge, and this pleasantness is not totally separate from the fantasy of dreams."[70]

It is for precisely this reason that the Fathers enjoin asceticism—which is man's voluntary renunciation of the demands of the senses—as the only recommended way of using the world and at the same time the sole path to true knowledge of the world. When, for example, St Maximus the Confessor says that "all visible realities stand in need of the Cross,"[71] he is pointing to precisely this cross of self-renunciation of the individual will, as the only possibility for transcending the fantasy (in other words, the deception) of visible realities and knowing the truth of created things. An ascetic—non-consumerist—use of the world is presented as an ethical feat and a precondition for knowing the truth of cosmology and discovering its purpose and beauty.

In the writings of St Symeon the New Theologian too, particular stress is laid on an ascetic use of the world, which, in contrast to the consumerist use, saves the world itself and also man. This is why "absolute necessity for the body" is put forward as the measure and the "better way" in our use of the world. "Absolute necessity" is confined to the food, clothing, and shelter that man needs in order to survive.[72] If in addition to these man uses something more, then he should always feel it to be a particular blessing from God and believe that everything belongs to God, and He provides everything.[73]

It is only when man has come to see the world in this way and acquired the genuine criteria that such a way of seeing affords, that he can start thinking about ways to protect the world and to work creatively in it. The "tilling and keeping" of the commandment which Genesis sets before us is to be interpreted today as the task

70 Letter 4, *Ascetic Works*, ed. Spanos, p. 389.
71 *First Century on Theology* 67, PG 90.1108B.
72 Cf. 1 Tim 6:8: "...if we have food and clothing, with these we shall be content."
73 *Catechetical Orations* 2, SC 96, p. 272; cf. Ps 144:16: "Thou openest Thy hands, Thou satisfiest the desire of every living thing."

of preserving the world which is incumbent upon every Christian. The holier a person is and the more his life is governed by the spirit of asceticism, the more clearly he sees the dangers which threaten life today and the harder he works in his own sphere to overcome them. For instance, the pressing need to lead the economic development of our day to something beyond itself, and the equally pressing need for today's closed materialistic system to go beyond itself, opening up to realities not defined only by matter—Christians always have an obligation to point such things out and impress them on the international consciousness as primary needs, principally by their own lives.[74]

Asceticism in Orthodox spiritual life is understood as the essential and unceasing effort on the Christian's part to gain the ability to distinguish the positive from the negative and take what is positive into his life; it is impossible to separate the good from the bad with sense-organs which are seeking after pleasure. Hence a participation in the good things of creation which is aesthetic, discriminating, and with fear of God is distinguished from, and opposed to, an indiscriminate and "pleasure-ful" use of these things, precisely because the latter does not know the limits of need and is "pregnant with fear of death"[75] and brings about man's alienation. Thus asceticism and the ascetic struggle mean from one point of view resistance to alienation; in other words, man's refusal to evaporate into the surrounding consumerist atmosphere of hedonism and pursuit of happiness like a droplet of the same stuff. For man, there is no more tragic form of alienation than using and partaking of God's creations and good things without thanksgiving and communion with Him. This alienation is characterized by stubborn ignorance of God— despite the richness of His gifts—and contains all the pain of man's separation from God and the deadness that goes with deprivation of the true life. As St

74 Cf. P. Nellas, "Christians in the World," p. 21.
75 Cf. Symeon the New Theologian, *Chapters* 3.17, SC 51, p. 128.

Symeon underlines in this connection, people who are ignorant of God may revel in pleasures with their bodily senses and delight in the good things of creation like dumb animals, but they are unable to discern God as Creator and Bestower of all these things and are thus deprived of everything good.[76]

Egotism and self-love are passions which find particularly fertile ground in the person who is consumeristic, intemperate, and hedonistic. So we understand why St Symeon stresses that material goods should be partaken of not only with thanksgiving to God, but also with temperance, avoiding satiety and excess.[77] By an ascetic use of the world, man in practice renounces his egocentricity and his demand to subjugate everything to his individual self-interest. He loves and respects his environment and does not attempt to translate its value into impersonal money—i.e. into objective units of utilitarian use—but regards everything around him as *pragmata, things resulting from action* by a personal creator and God.[78] So when man sees material goods not as consumer items and objects but as results of action by God's love, he has the possibility of transfiguring them through his entire life into events of personal relationship and communion. Then this relationship with the world becomes an indirect relationship with the Maker of the world, with God, while the practical ascetic use of the world becomes an unceasing study in the truth of the world—an education which no rationalistic research or "exact"

76 "For what could be worse than being parted from Thee, O Savior?
    What more painful than to be separated from life
    and thence to live like a corpse, deprived of life,
    and be deprived of all good things at once?
    For one who is parted from Thee, is deprived of all good;
    for now those who do not know Thee enjoy bodily pleasures
    here, and are happy, gambolling like dumb beasts,
    having the things that Thou hast given for enjoyment in this life,
    and seeing only these..." (*Hymns* 1, SC 156, p. 164)

77 *Catechetical Orations* 26, SC 113, p. 82.

78 Translator's note: the noun *pragma*, "a thing," derives from the verb *pratto*, "to make or do."

science can provide. Especially in these days of unrestrained exploitation, abuse, and violation of the environment, the ascetic and non-consumerist ethos put forward by the Fathers is particularly salutary, since it shows how man should restrict his acquisitive appetites towards nature in order to find himself more truly and organically connected with it, as he was created by God to be.

It would be an omission not to mention that the ascetic and non-consumerist use of the world also works towards social justice and the restitution of goods to people to whom they equally belong, but who are deprived of them. Greed, avarice, and consumerist living, which form a basic cause of social injustice, have no place in the life of the true Christian, who should be self-sufficient in the sense of restricting his needs to real necessities. His life should be regulated by temperance and not by luxury, consumerism, extravagance, and the superfluous pseudo-needs which are created by people who have "the spirit of this world" in order to justify all that they possess as providing for their "necessities."[79] The natural things of the world are in God's ownership. God has given them in common to all human beings, granting people the right of use only, the purpose being for everyone to provide for their needs, and not for people to bring things into their possession and make them a permanent acquisition.[80] This view finds a place in the more general ascetic spirit of Orthodoxy which should characterize the

---

79 Fictitious needs are rejected and judged severely by the Fathers. See Basil, *To the Rich* 2, PG 31.284A-285B. Also John Chrysostom, *On Ephesians* Hom. 2.4, PG 62.22, where a comparison is made between moderation and excess, with concrete examples. This position of the Fathers in rejecting false and superfluous "needs" corresponds to the cultivation of the non-consumerist spirit today. In a variety of ways, and especially through advertising and the great possibility of choice, man is pushed into consumption and the creation of artificial "needs" which do not actually serve him, but serve rather the logic and the purposes of commercial gain. The non-consumerist spirit is a clear reaction against this logic. It is to be understood in the context of an effort to change the economy from an instrument of profiteering and exploitation to an instrument serving human needs. See I. Petrou, *Social Justice* (in Greek) (Thessaloniki, 1968), p. 160.

80 *Catechetical Orations* 9, SC 104, 110-112.

lives of all the faithful and lead them to a right use of the things in the world. Such use has as its purpose provision for basic material needs and does not deteriorate into misuse or abuse of the world.

Here it should be underlined that the notion of "God's steward" used by the Fathers does not have a dogmatic flavor and should not be connected with a projection onto God of the unequal distribution of material goods.[81] The unequal distribution is due to humans who have disrupted God's original equality. So starting from this state of affairs which was shaped by humans and exists in human society, the Fathers talk about man as the steward of God so that they can go on to use this proposition as an argument in their effort to persuade the rich to give their surplus wealth to the poor.[82]

Again, beside man's rights over nature there is also nature's "right" over man, which dictates a direct link between man's economic rights and his basic ecological obligations. Thus the level of man's economic rights cannot be increased at will in line with his increasing demands, because economic growth has ecological limits. Man's struggle for survival cannot be carried on at the expense of nature, since if it is, the ecological death of the earth will put an end to human life too.[83] Human rights in the economic sphere need to be harmonized with the basic ecological preconditions for the survival of humanity in its natural environment. They cannot be realized through unchecked economic growth, but only through a growth which is accompanied by economic justice within the framework of the "limits of growth." Economic justice, which consists in the disposal and distribution of the goods necessary for living, of natural resources and

---

81 Basil, *To the Rich* 3, PG 31.288B; *idem., On "I will pull down my barns"* 2 and 7, PG 31.264C and 276; John Chrysostom, *On Lazarus* 2.5, PG 48.988; *On Genesis* 35.8, PG 53.331-2; *On 1 Corinthians* 10.3, PG 61.85-86; Symeon, *Catechetical Orations* 9, SC 104, pp. 110-112.

82 See I. Petrou., *op. cit.,* pp. 53-54.

83 For several years now, these fears have been expressed on many sides and at many levels. See for example P. Samuel, *Ecologie: détente ou cycle infernal* (Paris, 1973).

industrial means of production, needs to address itself to the survival and common life of people and nations. In this way it is possible to achieve ecological stability in coexistence and common life with "non-rational" creation. Economic and ecological justice presuppose each other, and as such can only be achieved together.[84] Furthermore, this linking of economic and ecological problems is presupposed also in the New Testament view of the subject, where the term *oikonomia* ("economy" or "stewardship") has the same sense as the modern term "ecology,"[85] which denotes the management, administration and care for the things of the household with attentiveness and frugality.[86]

4. The example of monasticism

The inner principle of created things is not simply their "meaning," the "idea" of each entity, but the being of things as this is revealed as "life personified and life-force,"[87] in other words as the operation of the Holy Spirit. Hence also the beauty of created things (not the aesthetic beauty of fantasy, but the beauty which is revealed to the person who is purified and crucified to the passions) reflects the personal character of the divine energy which manifests itself as Trinitarian, being at the same time unified and undivided.[88] This truth is manifested as a living reality in natural

84 See J. Moltmann, "Theologische Begründung der Menschenrechte," p. 173.

85 Translator's note: In the popular, rather than the scientific sense.

86 See Lk 12:42.

87 Maximus the Confessor, *On Various Difficulties*, PG 90.296D: "From the natural movement of beings we learn of the personified life of the being, the life-force of beings, the Holy Spirit." See also *idem, Centuries on Theology* PG 90.1209A: "The Holy Spirit is in all things in a manner which is simple, inasmuch as He is that which holds all things together and exercises providence for them, and sets in motion the seminal potentialities in their nature."

88 See Athanasius, *Letter 3*, To Serapion, 45, PG 26.632BC: "For the Father creates all things through the Word, in the Spirit, since where the Word is, there is the Spirit also; and the things created through the Word have the power of being from the Spirit by the Word." See also Ps 32:6, "By the word of the Lord the heavens were made, and all their power by the Spirit of His mouth."

contemplation, which is a specific ascetic way involving renunciation of self-love and purification from the passions, through which man becomes able to approach the beauty of the world personally and have direct and tangible experience of the true dimensions of the world. The ultimate end of Christian cosmology—of natural contemplation—is the unification of "all in all" in the singular uniqueness of the divine life. This means that natural contemplation is consummated in the vision of God and in true theology, which is deification and experience of the uncreated inner principle of the divine energies, in the ever-moving motionlessness and still movement of the "contemplative life" as it is expressed principally in Orthodox monasticism.

Monasticism, especially in its coenobitic form, is often held up by the Fathers as an example of a society which preserves truth, authenticity, and respect in the monks' relations with each other and also with the world around them.[89] Since in Orthodox theology asceticism is not thought of as an aversion to matter and the world or a rejection of the bodily value of the person, but as transcendence of man's individuality, then monastic life too cannot be taken as anti-material and anti-nature, or as contributing to the disruption of the normal relationship between the spiritual and the material—despite various misunderstandings at different times. The charismatic and "spirit-bearing" monk does not maltreat material things and the environment, but looks after them and respects them. For this reason, in ascetic use and in the ascetic life of the monk the world is restored to its original beauty. In Orthodox monasteries, one sees quite clearly the unity and conjunction of spirit and matter. Spiritual life is not separated from the rest of life, nor is material food separated from spiritual. The

---

89 Basil, *Ascetic Instructions* 18.1-2, PG 31.1381C-1384A. Alongside the monastic coenobium, certainly, the community held up by other Fathers as an ideal society is the original church community in Jerusalem, which was characterized by a similar way of life. See *idem, In Famine and Drought* 8, PG 31.325AB, and John Chrysostom, *On Acts* 7.2, PG 60.65.

material construction and decoration of the monastery is done in a manner that is spiritual, while the spiritual life carried on there has absolute respect for the material aspect of humans and for their natural environment. In the refectory, where the monks take their physical nourishment, an exceptionally reverent and spiritual atmosphere is created which effortlessly makes the point that the time spent there is an extension of the Office and the Divine Liturgy. At the beginning and end of the meal there is a blessing with the appropriate prayer, while during the meal the monks, and pilgrims who are staying with them, are spiritually nourished with readings from homilies of the Fathers or the Synaxarion for the Saint of the day. Nourished with the blessed material food, they are fortified and grow spiritually and are led to give thanks and glory to God.[90]

It is characteristic that while St Symeon the New Theologian more than any other extols the monastic life, he does not restrict man's destiny and salvation to this, or make it an absolute. On the contrary, he believes that one can "attain to perfection of the virtues"[91] not only in the desert and in monasticism but also in the world, which is characterized particularly by the cares of daily life. Spiritual life is not defined geographically and objectively by the world, the coenobium, or the desert, but by faith and love for Christ. As proof and witness to this truth we have all those saints who were well-pleasing to God while living in the world.[92]

Corresponding to this is the position Symeon takes regarding the form of monastic life. Though a cenobitic monk himself, he accepts that within monasticism there are different ways leading to God. Thus monastic life may be either eremitic or coenobitic, or even related to the pastoral work of the Church: "presiding

---

90 See further Archimandrite Vasileios of Stavronikita [now Iviron], *Theological Commentary on the Frescoes*, pp. 45-48.

91 *Catechetical Orations* 22, SC 104, pp. 364-392.

92 *Catechetical Orations* 7, SC 104, pp. 64-66.

over the people, admonishing and teaching and organizing Churches." He does not recommend any one of these ways or express a particular preference, since all of them afford the possibility of living "for God and in accordance with God."[93] Just as the life of a human society consists of various branches of knowledge and crafts and requires each person to make their contribution through their own trade in order to provide for the material needs of the community as a whole, the same happens in spiritual matters: all believers should assist towards the same goal through the gift that each possesses and the path he follows.[94]

It should also be emphasized that in Orthodox theology there is no dichotomy between society and the desert, nor any dualism or polarization within creation. The whole of creation exists as a work made by God and the place of His "dominion."[95] But while every place is able to be a "place of God's dominion," it can also deteriorate into a place of demonic tyranny. There are not a few instances where neptic Fathers see the desert as an area that can become a dwelling place of the devil—a place that is under the arbitrary domination and operation of antichrist. In this case, however, the ascetics do not hesitate to go into the territory of the enemy and do battle with him, cleansing the place and giving it back to the Creator. On the other hand, the monk believes that it is not only the devil, but also man's sin that pollutes a place.[96] As Abba John used to say, "My sons, let us not make this place dirty, since our Fathers cleansed it from the demons."[97] By his asceticism and struggle, the monk "guards the place." Thus the desert

93 *Chapters* 3.65, SC 51, p. 160.
94 *Chapters* 3.66, SC 51, p. 160.
95 Ps 102:22; but it is most especially the following Psalm, 103, the opening Psalm at Vespers, that underlines the truth that God's creative presence extends throughout creation.
96 "I have become... a pollution to air and earth and water"; *Oktoekhos*, Tone 7, Monday, second *stikhera* at Vespers.
97 John the Eunuch, 5; *Sayings of the Desert Fathers: The Alphabetical Collection*, tr. Benedicta Ward SLG (London and Kalamazoo, 1975), p. 90.

ceases to signify an absence of true communion and love or the domination of individuality and fragmentation—i.e. of the devil—but is instead the place that is taken up by the body of the Church and is now in indissoluble relationship with it.

The monks project by their lives a dynamic way of dealing with creation and using it that does away with any sort of absolute divisions into sacred and profane. Palladius of Helenopolis, the author of the *Lausiac History*, relates the following incident: one day when he went to draw water from the well, he saw a reptile in there and returned empty handed to his elder, Abba Dorotheos. The latter then said to him, "If it seems good to the devil to put snakes or reptiles or other venomous beasts into all the springs of water, are you going to go without ever drinking?" And when he had drawn water from the well himself and drunk it, he added, "Where the Cross descends, the malice of Satan has no force."[98] In this case, we see that the devil did not operate through his personal presence, but tried by means of creation (the reptile) to make creation (the water) autonomous vis-à-vis man. The ascetics, however, cleanse the creation that satan has polluted, not recognizing his occupancy of any part of it. This cleansing manifests a liturgical relation between man and the world. Man and the world are not two self-existent, objective realities, but man is the priest who brings into Holy-trinitarian communion the creation, which had lost that communion at the Fall.[99]

So creation cannot be divided into two areas static by nature, with given and opposite characteristics, the desert and the world; but it is an observation common to the theology of the Fathers and that of St Symeon the New Theologian that in the desert and the world equally, the demons make an effort to alienate man and change creation by deflecting man's "godly purpose."[100] The

98 PG 34.1011D-1012A.
99 See Thanasis Papathanasiou, "The Anchoretic Life" (in Greek), *Synaxi* 13 (1985), p. 39.
100 *Chapters* 1.22, SC 51, p. 52.

world is regarded as particularly suitable for disorientating man from this purpose and as a sphere of demonic influence[101]—not, of course, the world as an actual place, but as a mentality and a spirit which governs those people who are obedient to the "prince of this world."[102] Hence for monks, renunciation of the world and complete withdrawal does not consist only in geographical separation, but functions principally as an exile from "all the materials and manners and opinions and persons in this life," as a denial of the carnal mind and above all of one's own will.[103] For while there are many who renounce the life of the world and the things that make it up, there are still few that progress to renunciation of their will and their desires.[104]

The monk's relationship with the things of the world has a peculiar character. The monk comes from the world, but he lives "outside the camp" of the world. For this reason, he knows how to use the things around him with the awareness that they belong to this temporary, corruptible world.[105] Symeon the Studite, the New Theologian's elder who is referred to by his disciple as the model of a monk, was in the habit of saying that the monk should be "like someone who is and is not, who is not visible, or rather not even known"; which the New Theologian interprets to mean: present in the body, absent in the spirit, not visible except to those who have been purified by the Holy Spirit and not known "because he has nothing to do with anyone."[106] Thus the true monk remains dead and crucified to the world and the desires which the mind of the world arouses. Just as someone who is outside a house cannot see the people inside it, so the monk, being

---

101 *Chapters* 1.15, SC 51, p. 48.
102 Jn 12:31.
103 *Chapters* 1.14, SC 51, p. 48.
104 *Chapters* 1.31, SC 51, p. 56. This is the interpretation Symeon gives to Mt 22:14, "Many are called, but few are chosen."
105 Gregory Palamas, Hom. 31, PG 151.388C.
106 *Catechetical Orations* 6, SC 104, p. 28.

"outside the camp" of the world and crucified and dead to the world, has no feeling of desire towards the things of the world.[107]

Yet the monk's attitude is not the result of coercion, but the fruit of free choice which gives meaning to the whole life of asceticism. The freedom of the ascetic monk remains an irreplaceable precondition for overcoming the desires dictated by the egocentricity of biological man, and for regarding existent things in a proper way.[108] The monk who has his thoughts revolving around care for the things of this life is not free, because he is enslaved and possessed by the worry of those thoughts. By contrast, one who is free does not worry about either himself or others in terms of the needs of this life, even if he happens to have some particular administrative task in the body of the Church, or if he is a bishop or an abbot or whatever else.[109]

The care of this life may be dismissed from the ascetic's life—in other words, the constant and persistent preoccupation with the provision of goods which often go to satisfy the greed of biological man; but this does not mean that he also rejects that use of the good things of creation which is based on moderation and discernment. The monk's freedom from care does not imply disdain, neglect, or abhorrence for creation and the good things which God offers us through it.[110] An excellent standard for the monk's freedom from care—interpreted not as a passive state but as trust in God's love—combined with admiration for the beauty and value of nature, is provided by the Gospel in the Sermon on the Mount,[111] where Christ refers to the birds of the air and the lilies of the field.

---

107 *Chapters* 3.36, SC 51, p. 40.

108 *Chapters* 1.37, SC 51, p. 60.

109 *Chapters* 1.81, SC 51, p. 88.

110 "But nor will the monk ever be idle or despise anything, even the meanest and smallest of things; but doing everything and acting always in a way pleasing to God, he will be free from care in everything and in the whole of life." *Chapters* 1.81, SC 51, p. 88.

111 Mt 6:25-28.

Through his ascetic life and his daily struggle, the monk attains to what is called spiritual knowledge of existent things. This is a "charismatic" state, a state of grace, having attained which, the humble and ascetic monks stand amazed at the spectacle of the revelation of God's wonders. Thus while they sit in the common monastic refectory with all the rest of the brotherhood, to their intellect all the good things that their eyes see seem like a shadow, while their taste even ceases to sense the sweetness of the foods. St Symeon the New Theologian particularly underlines the fact that it is the Grace of God that shows things to them in this way. So as they see the things that God has made and have personal assurance and experience of the inertia and corruption of sensible things, these Spirit-bearing monks do not show loathing for these things or reject them, but "graft" their fear of becoming enslaved to sensible things onto love and yearning for spiritual things. This "grafting," which constitutes spiritual knowledge and conveys man imperceptibly and safely from fear of sensible things to love of intelligible things, is an intermediate stage between those two states.[112] Here it should be noted that dispassion is understood in the Orthodox patristic tradition not as mortification of the affective part of the soul, but as a possibility of transmuting it and turning it into an energy pleasing to God and a yearning for God.[113]

Asceticism unifies the monk himself and restores his cognitive functions to their original purity and working order. At the same time, it contributes to the restoration and perfection of his direct

---

112 *Chapters* 1.32, SC 51, p. 58: "When you sit with the whole brotherhood in the refectory and in the perception of your intellect everything is sketched before your eyes as a shadow, and you do not perceive the sweetness of the food, but your whole soul is amazed at the wonder and filled with tears, know then that the grace of your God is showing things to you in this way because of your great humility that comes through fear; so that when you see the things that God has made and learn of the inertia of sensible things, you may graft your fear onto love of things intelligible. And this is the spiritual knowledge that you hear spoken of, which is a mean between fear and love and conveys man from the one to the other imperceptibly and safely."

113 See Gregory Palamas, *In Defence of the Holy Hesychasts* 2.2.19; Chrestou, vol. 1, p. 526. See also *Hagioretic Tome*, PG 150.1233B.

relationship with the things around him. This change is consummated in the realm of worship and prayer, where the monk becomes transparent and open to God and the world. The life of asceticism, prayer, and sanctification elevate the monk into a workshop in which the world is transformed into Church. By his life, the charismatic monk calls the things of the world to become holy things, and the whole world to become Church. His relationship with all creations is wholly one of love. He gathers the shattered world into his love and brings it into the Church, opening it up to the healing energy of the Grace of God. This love of his is expressed in an infinite tenderness which takes hold of his heart and makes it unable to bear the slightest pain inflicted on any creature. He is moved by a boundless compassion for the whole of nature which increasingly breaks down into paroxysms of love, as the monk journeys towards the "likeness of God" and deification.

Lives of the Saints refer to an unusual sympathy and compassion for animals, plants and in general every creature—unusual not just in the everyday behavior of people in the world, but also by the standards of monastic life, which in other ways is so harsh. This is a sympathy and a compassion which are not manifestations of pathological sentimentalism, but reveal a true supra-natural greatness. These Saints believed that any misuse or ill-treatment of nature is contrary to the will of God. St Silouan the Athonite, for instance, used to say that "the Divine Spirit teaches sympathy for all creation" and stressed that "the heart that has learnt to love is sorry for all created things."[114] But this love was combined in the saint himself with the most realistic approach to the things of this world. As a genuine monk, he knew that everything was created in order to serve man, who "may make use of everything when necessary."[115] At the same time, he emphasizes the

---

114 Archimandrite Sophrony, *St Silouan the Athonite* (Crestwood, 1999), p. 94.

115 *Ibid.* As his biographer notes, "he would scythe hay, fell trees, stock up with wood for the winter, eat fish" (p. 95). He did not eat meat because, as is well known, on Athos the coenobitic monks and hermits do not as a rule eat meat, in accordance

danger of becoming attached to the things of nature and especially to animals, an attachment that often goes so far as to be "friendship," which he regarded as "a perversion of the order established by God and contrary to the normal state of man" as he was first created. Yet "harm done unnecessarily to an animal—to plant life, even—gainsays the law of Grace. But attachment to animals likewise goes against the divine commandment."[116]

The lives of the great hermits and monks show the tremendous repercussions that the ascetic life has for society and its potential for providing examples. The holiness of the monks is the essential precondition for their true and proper relationship both with created things and with the uncreated God,[117] while the witness and message of their life is that only the ascetic and non-consumerist use of the world can save man and the world: "Indeed nothing is better in the world, brethren, than to have no part in the world, and not to want anything more than the basic necessities for the body."[118]

Especially definitive for the monk's relationship with the things of the world is the meaning and significance that these things take on in the realm of fallenness and sin. For those things which serve to provide for bodily needs are used by monks too, while a sinful and impassioned relationship with these things is avoided in their lives. This, indeed, is the meaning of the monk's withdrawal from the world.[119] This is why our holy Father sees the

with the words of the Apostle, "If food is a cause of my brother's falling, I will never eat meat" (1 Cor 8:13).

116 Archimandrite Sophrony, *St Silouan the Athonite*, pp. 95-96.

117 *Chapters* 2.7, SC 51, p. 106.

118 *Catechetical Orations* 2, SC 96, p. 272.

119 "For this is true withdrawal from the world and the things in the world: to hate and abhor the things of the world once one has left the world. But what is the world, and what are the things in it? Listen! It is not gold, or silver, or horses, or mules: for we too have all of these, as much as we require to serve our bodily needs. It is not meat, or bread, or wine; for we too partake of these and eat of them in moderation. It is not houses, or baths, or country properties, or vineyards, or estates; for the lavras and monasteries are made up of these. So what is 'the world'? It is sin,

love and attachment that certain monks have for the things of the world as especially tragic, precisely because these things become autonomous and surpass their love for Christ.[120] The tendency to accord autonomy and absolute value to material things, which can find its way even into the lives of monks, has very tragic consequences for them. This is why even the material things, which in the lives of many monks who attain holiness often receive grace and are sanctified—their monastic clothing, for instance—can lead others to destruction, if they are made autonomous from God.[121]

Monks do not reject or despise material goods. Nevertheless, their ascetic attitude towards these things is dictated not only by the distinction between need and luxury which characterizes the choices and the criteria in their lives, but also by a deep sense of sinfulness and the continuous experience of repentance which constrains their hearts. St Symeon assures us that he has known monks who deprived themselves even of inexpensive foods because they lived with humility, contrition, and consciousness of their own sinfulness.[122] At the age of fourteen Symeon himself, with the aid of his spiritual father Symeon the Studite "who trampled underfoot the powers of the devil in the guise of the passions," began to tread this path of monastic life as a process of going out of the "world" and getting away from the influence of the "world ruler," the devil. Again, it is not fortuitous that in some of his writings he metaphorically calls the fallen world "Egypt," and the devil "Pharaoh."[123]

Another factor which dictates a non-consumerist attitude to material goods on the part of the monk, and the acceptance of

attachment to things, and passions." *Catechetical Orations* 5, SC 96, pp. 438-40. Cf. Jn 13:23 and 1 Jn 2:15-16.

120 *Catechetical Orations* 3, SC 96, p. 286.

121 *Catechetical Orations* 29, SC 113, p. 188.

122 *Catechetical Orations* 12, SC 104, p. 174: "I know that there are some of you sitting here in our midst, contrite in spirit and humble in mind, who refrain even from these cheap foods in the refectory, thinking themselves unworthy to partake of them."

123 *Hymns* 17, SC 174, p. 86.

such goods with thanksgiving, is the fact that egotism and self-love are passions which flourish especially in the person who is consumeristic, intemperate, and hedonistic. For this reason, St Symeon the New Theologian advises monks not to examine the portions of food put out in the refectory (to see which is larger and which is smaller) but to accept whatever is offered to them with thanksgiving to God, with temperance, and avoiding satiety.[124] For the monk, reception of the good things of creation in a way that is eucharistic—with thanksgiving—must have its starting-point in the constant remembrance of the goodness and long-suffering of God who gives him all good things—food, water, clothing, shelter, and even his cell "for the body's enjoyment."[125] In monastic life especially, the saving attitude towards all material goods is always a rational use of them, while at the same time avoiding the "desire of the flesh," the "desire of the eyes," and the "vain boasting of the thoughts." This is the attitude maintained by all the saints who passed their lives in perfect holiness while living amidst the things of the world and its cares.[126]

Finally, the monks bear witness to the fact that freedom from care does not mean rejection of the created world. On the other hand, affirming materiality does not necessarily mean affirming sin, just as rejection and contempt for God's good things in this life cannot be equated with desire for eternal and heavenly good things. This is because quite simply, as our holy Father emphasizes, there are many who despise the former but few who care about the latter.[127] The true, charismatic monk uses material goods as gifts and blessings, in order to express the glory and

---

124 *Catechetical Orations* 26, SC 113, p. 82.

125 *Catechetical Orations* 30, SC 113, p. 202.

126 *Catechetical Orations* 5, SC 96, pp. 440-2. Cf. 1 Cor 7:29-31.

127 *Chapters* 1.88, SC 51, p. 94: "Not desiring the delightful and sweet things of the world is not the same as longing for eternal and invisible good things; one is different from the other. For many have despised the former, but few people have taken care for the latter."

greatness of God. It is not by chance that it was within monasticism that liturgical art developed—architecture, iconography, hymnography, music, embroidery, etc.—the achievements of which lead man to give glory to God. Only in the context of asceticism, cultivated *par excellence* in monasticism, is a true art able to flower. Before the material world can be used as an expression of God's glory, man's intellect needs to be changed and transfigured by the Grace of God. But this requires serving time in asceticism and renewing man's intellect by continuous repentance. This is the reason why it is incumbent upon monasticism to stand as an example of how to take up the good things of creation in a way that is non-consumerist and eucharistic, and to embody the "alternative ethos" and the true relationship between man and creation.

5

THE TRANSFIGURATION OF THE
WORLD IN CHRIST

1. *The Incarnation of Christ as starting point for the restoration of the world*

In an earlier chapter, we saw how the Fall led man to misuse creation and treat it as autonomous, despite the fact that by virtue of his natural makeup he had the power, as microcosm and mediator, to "make it word." But it was impossible for the Creator in His goodness to abandon His creature to the corruption of his fall. Man lost life, but God gave him the possibility of survival. Man destroyed the selfless and ingenuous relationship which he had had with the world, but was given the possibility of finding his food by cultivating the earth with sweat and labor; in other words, the possibility of work. He refused a direct knowledge of things in the light of grace, but was given the possibility of a new, indirect knowledge to be cultivated through science. In His measureless love for mankind, God transformed the result of sin into an occasion for blessing and gave man another chance. This is the reality of the garments of skin, in other words the new state in which man finds himself after the Fall thanks to God's loving and compassionate intervention.[1] This state allows man to survive, with a view to his

---

1   Gen 3.21. On interpretation of the garments of skin see Gregory the Theologian, Or. 45 *On the Holy Pascha*, 8, PG 36.633A; Gregory of Nyssa, *Oration on those who have fallen asleep*, PG 46.524D-532C; Maximus the Confessor, *On Various Questions of Ss Dionysius and Gregory*, PG 91.1304-1313B, and *To Thalassius*, PG 90:436AB; Gregory Palamas, Homily 31, PG 151.388C; Nicholas Kavasilas, *The*

complete redemption and salvation in Christ. It is an intermediate state in which the initial dynamism of creation continues to operate, albeit in a disorientated and distorted form. Human freedom begins to play a decisive role, with the result that evil is tragically active.

On the other hand, God has never ceased to intervene, calling and guiding His world, and above all, His chosen people. But the most decisive and irrevocable intervention was His Incarnation, in which He assumed the whole human state except for sin. Thus the task which has its starting point in man's natural capacity for being a mediator between God and the world and which is fulfilled in the deification of man, namely the return of the world to the beauty in which it was first created and the full interpenetration of created and uncreated—this task was not carried through by the first Adam. But it was accomplished in the person of the second Adam, Christ, who became the first father of the "new creation."[2]

The fact of the Incarnation of the Son and Word of God is pivotal to the Christian faith. Scripture describes it as the central event in creation and in history. It is the evangelist John the Theologian above all who stresses its significance and importance, speaking of the creative Word of God through whom "all things were made." This Word is the life and light of the whole creation,[3] and it is proclaimed concerning Him that "the Word was made flesh."[4] The term "flesh" here confirms not only the mystery of the divine Incarnation, but also the value of the material substance of the entire creation. All things in creation acquire substance, meaning, and purpose as material and bodily things, since,

---

Life in Christ 1, PG 150.508A-516B. On patristic teaching concerning the garments of skin see also P. Nellas, *Deification in Christ*, tr. N. Russell (Crestwood, 1987), pp. 43-91.

2   Maximus the Confessor, *Various Questions*, PG 91.1308D-1312B.

3   Jn 1:1-5.

4   Jn 1:14.

as the Apostle Paul writes, in Him all things whether visible or invisible hold together.[5]

This dimension of the divine Incarnation is noted by St Symeon the New Theologian. In His Incarnation the Son and Word of God became what He was not, a man like us, having all the characteristics of a human being except for sin, and being seen by all as God-man.[6] The Word of God is not some idea or theoretical principle, but a hypostasis, a person. The Word became man at a time when man had already proceeded to desecrate creation by making it into a god and worshipping it; and this, as we have already seen, is the ultimate defilement and corruption of God's pure work. God came down to earth in order to give life back to man, to recall him from error, and to help him restore his relationship with the environment.[7]

It is a principle of patristic thought and theology that anthropology and cosmology are presented within a christological framework. In this case, the Mother of God is taken as the bridge between God and creation. Thus St Symeon the New Theologian makes a parallel between Adam's already living side, out of which Eve was created, and the living flesh of the Mother of God which, like a piece of leaven taken from humanity, caused the unapproachable and incomprehensible Divinity of the Creator to be united with the whole "dough" of human nature.[8] God the Word took flesh from the Mother of God, and in return gave her the Holy Spirit. Through the Holy Spirit, He gave life to her most spotless soul, "raising her up from death." This was done because Eve had been the first to be given over to spiritual death. By His Incarnation the Word became

5 Col 1:16-17.
6 *Hymns* 51, SC 196, p. 190:
   "...and (the Son) became what He was not, a man like me,
   apart from sin and without transgression,
   seen by all as both God and man."
7 *Ethical Discourses* 1.2, SC 122, pp. 192-194; *On the Mystical Life,* vol. 1, pp. 30-31.
8 *Ethical Discourses* 1.3, SC 122, pp. 194-6; *On the Mystical Life,* vol. 1, p. 31.

man, "acquiring in Himself a body with a mind and a soul." He took on the same living flesh of Adam and the Mother of God, in order to renew the whole of human nature. At His birth according to the flesh He entered the world in order to seek and refashion Adam and the whole of creation.[9] This was done with respect for human freedom. He deified the created element which the Virgin had offered voluntarily, thereby opening the way for man to be deified and the whole creation to be renewed.[10]

Nevertheless, if creation is to be renewed, its dynamism has to rediscover its proper orientation and its authentic mode of functioning and reach its true purpose. This task depends on man's freedom and his willingness to "conceive" and "incarnate" the Word of God in his life. St Symeon speaks of this possibility for believers, especially the saints, to conceive and bear the Word of God "similarly" to the Mother of God,[11] and also of how deified people are akin to the Mother of God in three ways.[12] After the Incarnation of the Word another kinship and relationship is created, not just between man and God but also between human beings themselves. This kinship, moreover, is a prerequisite if humans are to live in the right way.[13]

9   *Ethical Discourses* 2.7, SC 122, pp. 380-2; *On the Mystical Life*, vol. 1, pp. 112-3.

10 See G. Florovsky, "The Idea of Creation in Christian Philosophy," in *Eastern Churches Quarterly* 8, 3 (1949), p. 56ff.

11 The tenth chapter of the First Ethical Discourse is entitled: "That all the saints conceive in themselves the Word of God similarly to the Mother of God, and give birth to Him, and He is born in them and they are born of Him; and that they are His sons and brothers and mothers..." SC 122, p. 252.

12 SC 122, p. 264; *On the Mystical Life*, vol. 1, p. 60: "The saints therefore are triply her kin: first, in that they are related to her from the same clay and breath of life [given Adam]; secondly, that they have communion and share with her in the flesh which was taken from her; thirdly and last, that on account of the hallowing that has come to pass in them through her by virtue of the Spirit, each conceives in like manner to her within himself the God of all, as she bore Him in herself. For, if indeed she gave birth to Him in the body, yet she always possessed all of Him in the spirit, and has Him now, and will ever have Him inseparable from her."

13 *Ethical Discourses* 1.5, SC 122, p. 228.

Yet while the principle purpose of the Incarnation of the Word is to bring man back to a state in accordance with nature[14] and to deify him, the remainder of creation is not left out of its renewing power either. Since all things were created through the Word of God,[15] it follows that everything is subject to His work of renewal. And while it appears that this work is anthropocentric in character and, initially at least, concerns man, its meaning and reality are universal and embrace "all things."[16] When man is made new in Christ, the whole of creation is renewed with him. A new creation means being re-created in a dynamic relationship with the Creator-Word of all existent things (i.e. a relationship not only with God, but also with nature as His creation). In this case, creation is presented as a living unity which unfolds and is renewed together with man through his re-creative synergy with the creative work of God. Again, this is why the moral responsibility arising from this understanding of renewal and the obligation it places on each human being is tremendous, because our work has the potential to be part of God's work of renewal.[17]

All created things are a manifestation of the love of the Creator Word. They are "letters" which speak of Him in a language common to all people.[18] But at least in the context of the Orthodox Church and her theology, the Incarnation of the Word cannot be understood as an isolated event unrelated to the rest of life, but rather as a revelation of the love of God who comes to deliver and transfigure man, and with him the whole created universe. Christ, "in whom the whole fullness of deity dwells

14   *Chapters* 3.88, SC 51, pp. 176-8.
15   Col 1:16: "All things were created through Him and for Him."
16   In this connection, see 2 Cor 5:17: "If anyone is in Christ, he is a new creation; the old has passed away, behold, the new has come."
17   Cf. Nissiotis, *op. cit.*, p. 18.
18   Maximus the Confessor, *On Various Difficulties*, PG 91.1285D. "For having ineffably hidden Himself for us in the inner principles (or "words") of existent things, He accordingly indicates Himself through each of the things that we see as through letters."

bodily,"[19] lovingly calls man, who had gone astray, to be deified, and nature that "groans and travails with him" (Rom 8:22) to be made new. Starting from the premise of God's love and His economy for man's sake in the Incarnation of the Word, one can understand why the whole of Scripture presents an indissoluble bond between man and nature. God's love and economy are in evidence again in the sequence according to which man and nature are made new. St Symeon the New Theologian's statements and reasoning on this subject are particularly characteristic and striking. At the creation, the environment was formed first and man followed; but in the re-creation and renewal which follows from the Incarnation of the Creator Word, man goes first and the rest of creation follows. Originally, the environment was made and adorned by God as a kingdom for Adam, for him to live in and enjoy. But if Christ had first renewed creation and made it incorruptible and eternal, what place would have been left for man to live in, "clothed in corruptible flesh" as he was?[20]

Creation, according to the Fathers, is inseparable from man and advances with him towards salvation. Its value is reckoned not solely from the fact that it exists for man's sake and aids his survival and development, but also from the fact that it serves as a "school for the knowledge of God"[21] and works for the edification

19 Col 2:9.
20 *Ethical Discourses* 2.7, SC 122, pp. 372-4; *On the Mystical Life,* vol. 1, p. 109: "When, however, He came who had created all things before and who now wished to renew them, he did not wish to renew them according to the same sequence by which He had created them before... Because, while He had then first prepared all the visible creation for Adam's habitation and enjoyment, as his kingdom, and then directly afterwards created man, now, on the other hand, if He had wanted first of all to renew creation and render it spiritual and incorruptible and eternal, where in that case would have the man have been able to dwell, clothed as he was in corruptible flesh, an animal and mortal? In what world then would he have been able to live, to marry and be married, to beget and be born, and to grow up? You have no answer, truly. So, for this reason God first raised up the man who had fallen, been broken and grown old, re-created and renewed him, and then subsequently the creation."
21 Basil, *Hexaemeron* I.6, PG 29.16C.

"and instruction of our souls."[22] Therefore God the Word in His Incarnation introduces the ineffable and life-giving operation of His divinity and His flesh into the deadly venom and the poison of sin which entered human life after the Fall, and with the human race He also delivers the rest of creation.[23] Living in the world as God-man, Christ restores man's harmonious relationship with God and also with creation. This relationship between man and creation in the new state which is in Christ acquires a soteriological character and eschatological content. After the coming of Christ into the world man still remains master of nature; but he has a duty always to manifest this mastery within the context of renewal and ultimate salvation, both his own and that of nature. This is why the fact of God's becoming man is the starting point *par excellence* for the restoration and renewal of nature. St Symeon develops this thesis with the aid of comparisons and parallels between Christ and Adam, and the Mother of God and Eve.[24] Making a comparison between the fall of man after his creation and the re-creation of man and the world, he stresses that with the Fall we observe divergence and discord between man and the world, while in the re-creation brought about through the Incarnation of the Word we have convergence and reconciliation.[25] Taking this point further, one could mention the vulgarity and lack of taste which even today characterize man's "renewal" and "embellishment" of creation when it is not open to communication with and reference to the work of renewal afforded by the Incarnation of God.

The christological basis of Orthodox cosmology and anthropology means that they are approached in the light of re-creation in Christ, which is the realization of the mystery of the divine

---

22 *Hexaemeron* IX.1, PG 29.189A.
23 *Catechetical Orations* 5, SC 96, p. 412.
24 See *Ethical Discourses* 2.7, SC 122, pp. 374-8; *On the Mystical Life,* vol. 1, p. 110.
25 See *Ethical Discourses* 2.7, SC 122, pp. 368-72.

economy for the salvation of man and the transfiguration of the
world. In consequence, man's relationship with creation has a
christological grounding and a soteriological perspective. Only in
this context does it have value and acquire content and purpose.
It is characteristic that in the hymnology for Christmas the unity
of man and creation, as well as the prospect of salvation for both,
are an evident reality. Man and creation are presented as united
through the fact of Christ's birth, and both in the same way show
their joy and gladness for the possibility of deliverance which
Christ's Incarnation gives.[26]

According to the theology of the Fathers, the Incarnation
brings about a new cosmogony in which "the bounds of nature
are overcome." Before the creation of the world, the Creator
knows about man's Fall and has in view the plan for his reshaping
and regeneration, to be carried out through the birth in the flesh
of God, His only Son. So in His power, compassion, and goodness He restrains and holds in check the impulse of all created
things, which did not want to accept Adam because of his Fall,
and at once makes them subject to man.[27] This is why the Incarnation of the Word is considered the starting point for the

26 See for example, "Mountains and hills, plains and ravines, people and races, nations
     and every breath, make a joyful noise, filled with godly merriment. For the deliver-
     ance of all has come to dwell here, the timeless Word of God, through pity become
     subject to time" (Sunday of the Forefathers, Kanon of the Forefeast, Ode 6). Char-
     acteristic of the hymn is the hymnographer's effort to include the whole of creation,
     inanimate and animate ("every breath") and the entire human race in the call to
     joy. Also characteristic is his theological stance, when he refers to the salvation of all
     things ("the deliverance of all") as a result of Christ's Incarnation. See further I.
     Galanis, "The Relationship between Man and Creation according to the New Tes-
     tament," pp. 392f.

27 "God who created all and made man, who knew before the world was made that
     Adam would transgress the commandment, and who had fore-ordained the man's
     rebirth and re-creation through the birth into the flesh of His only-begotten Son,
     what does God do here? He who holds all things together by His own power and
     compassion and goodness, now suspends the assault of all creation, and straightway
     subjects all of it to Adam as before." *Ethical Discourses* 1.2, SC 122, p. 190; *On the
     Mystical Life*, vol. 1, p. 29.

salvation and renewal of man and the world, while faith in Christ incarnate is characterized as a new paradise.[28]

But the Church Fathers see the renewal of creation in the light not only of the Incarnation of Christ, but also of His Resurrection—of that event which offers the new eschatological perspective which He created for the whole world. The Resurrection of Christ is the boundary-stone of the new creation. This is why Sunday, the day of the Resurrection, is characterized as the day of the re-creation of the world or the eighth day of creation.[29] By His Resurrection Christ has not only destroyed the power and operation of the devil "who had power over us because of death and sin";[30] He has also obtained for man the incorruption of his body and the renewal of material creation. Yet it is characteristic that Christ did not immediately give incorruption to the human body He had assumed; although He had divinized it by becoming man, He made it spiritual and incorruptible after His Resurrection. For in the same way as Adam experienced the death of his soul immediately after transgressing God's commandment but did not experience bodily death until many years later, so Christ in His Incarnation first raised up the soul and brought it to life and deified it, since the soul had been the first to receive as a penance the punishment of death. As for the body, which according to God's judgement pronounced at the time of the Fall[31] had to return to the earth through death, it was to enjoy incorruption through His Resurrection.[32] Again, when Christ descended into hell during

---

28 *Ethical Discourses* 2.7, SC 122, p. 386; *On the Mystical Life,* vol. 1, p. 114.

29 See Athanasius, *On the Sabbath and the Circumcision,* PG 28.133-141.

30 *Catechetical Orations* 5, SC 96, p. 412; cf. Lk 10:19 and Heb 2:14.

31 Gen 3:19.

32 *Ethical Discourses* 1.3, SC 122, p. 200; *On the Mystical Life,* vol. 1, p. 33: "Why did He not render the body right away spiritual and incorruptible with the soul when He assumed them both? This is because Adam, when he ate from the tree which God had forbidden him to eat of, suffered the death of his soul as soon as he transgressed, but that of the body only many years later. Christ therefore first raised up, vivified and deified the soul which had suffered first the punishment of death, and

His three-day burial, he freed the souls of the saints who were held there, raising them up and placing them in a place of repose and light that knows no evening; while He left their bodies to await incorruption in the general resurrection.[33] The relics of the saints give the clearest testimony possible to the sanctification and dignity afforded to the human body and to matter according to the measure of its participation in the life of the Resurrection.[34]

The Incarnation of God the Word marks the entry of the Holy Spirit into matter,[35] while His transfiguration manifests the consequence of the Incarnation, namely, that matter is renewed and filled with the Holy Spirit. If at the creation of the world the first organic life springs from matter at the Word of God,[36] the Incarnation testifies to His participation in matter. For this reason, when the Church had to confront the iconoclast view which disparaged matter and held that the believer's relationship with God is purely spiritual, she linked her teaching on icons with the Incarnation of God the Word, which, through the hypostatic union of the two natures, dignifies the whole man, with his sensible and spiritual components. "This is why Christ took a body and a soul," observes St John of Damascus: "—because man has a body and a soul."[37] Contemplating and seeing Christ with the mind alone would be a contradiction and betrayal of the reality of the Incarnation, through which He gave us the possibility of seeing

then, to the body condemned by the ancient judgement to return to the earth in death, he granted the reception of incorruptibility through the Resurrection."

33 *Ibid.*, Cf. Ezek 37:1ff.

34 *Hymns* 50, SC 196, p. 178.

35 Lk 1:35, "The Holy Spirit shall come upon thee..."

36 Gen 1:20, "Let the waters bring forth swarms of living creatures." The connection between matter and life becomes clearer at the making of man, where God is anthropomorphically presented as "taking dust from the earth" in order to create him.

37 *On Icons* 3.12, PG 64.1336B. See also *idem.*, *On the Orthodox Faith* 1.11, PG 94.844B. St Theodore the Studite, referring to the same iconoclastic view, points out: "If it were sufficient to behold Him in the intellect alone, then it would have been sufficient for Him to come to us in that way," *Antirrheticus* 1.7, PG 99.366D.

His face with our physical senses. Icons of Christ and of the saints are the best testimony to the participation of the sensible and material element in the immaterial and unseen spiritual reality. The Incarnation of God the Word proclaimed by the icon of Christ gives assurance of the inseparable unity of spirit and matter, and the dignity afforded to the latter in the one divine-human person of Christ. The ontological unity of God and man which Christ has established presupposes the material and sensible element.[38] St Symeon the New Theologian stresses that the reshaping and renewal of man and of all creation was brought about "through the bodily presence" of Christ.[39] Christ's body and His materiality are not illusory—just as man's spiritual nature is not merely notional— but are a tangible reality which gives man the possibility of ineffable transfiguration and true adoption.[40]

Over and above the renewal effected by God's becoming man, Christ Himself provided the measure and purpose of the relationship between man and creation through His teaching and example during His life on earth. The new element which is definitive for this relationship is that all the cares of everyday life must not be confined to material goods *per se* or to how we can manage or live well with them; rather, our care should be how to make man and the environment really part of the "Kingdom of God," which Christ Himself has inaugurated in the world. We have said that the renewal of nature requires that its dynamism should rediscover the

38 Here the sensible and material is united with God hypostatically and without confusion, i.e without ever becoming uncreated. See John of Damascus, *On the Divine Images* 1.16, PG 94.1245B. See further D. Tselengidis, *The Theology of the Icon and its Anthropological Significance* (in Greek) (Thessaloniki, 1984), p. 125.

39 *Ethical Discourses* 1.3, SC 122, p. 198; *On the Mystical Life*, vol. 1, pp. 32-33.

40 *Hymns* 50, SC 196, p. 170:
   "If He did not become body in fancy.
   then neither are we but notionally spirit;
   but as the Word was truly flesh
   so he ineffably transfigures us
   and makes us children of God in truth."

orientation, mode of functioning, and purpose proper to it. Through the whole of His life and particularly through His miracles, Christ showed this purpose, orientation, and functioning of nature. Miracles are not acts of magic; rather, they restore and perfect within things the inner principles (*logoi*) of those things, and the rationality of the world (i.e. its relation to *logos*). They are not magical operations by an all-powerful ruler who acts arbitrarily; rather, they restore to its natural way of functioning the creation which (furthermore) has been led by Christ to its end. Besides, in His teaching the Lord laid particular emphasis on this purpose, while in His Resurrection He broke the bonds of death and made the orientation more evident, the functioning possible, and the purpose attainable. Finally, the mission of His twelve disciples to the ends of the earth had the purpose of gathering together all things in Him, grafting them into His body that they might be "churched." This is why St Symeon speaks of the restoration and renewal of existent things before and after Christ became man.[41]

2. The "churching" of the world

The Church forms the potentiality for the entire world to be gathered together. This truth is presented and depicted with clarity in the iconography and architecture of an Orthodox church building. Participating simultaneously in the material and the spiritual world, man is able to form and give shape to matter in such a way that it retains the original orientation and purpose of its creation. Thus we have a "churching" of material creation and its participation in the glory of God—a characteristic of Byzantine art which we have described in earlier chapters.

On the basis of the thought of St Maximus the Confessor in particular, it has been said[42] that if the Church, which is the

---

41 *Catechetical Orations* 5, SC 96, pp. 412-4.

42 The argument of this paragraph is taken from N. Matsoukas, *World, Man and Communion*, pp. 219-222.

communion of rational and intelligible beings, did not exist, then creation would not be able to have knowledge of and conscious participation in the energies of God. This is to say that the entire structure that goes to make up creation forms the body of the Church: creation came into being for the Church. It can even be said that God created the Church as a symbol of Himself, His place and His image; for as St Maximus says, the Church is "an image and likeness of man who was created in the image and likeness of God."[43] Thus not only rational creation, but all the rest of creation too is able to relate to God and to maintain an indissoluble relationship with Him through the Church, which is the communion of all that exists. In St Maximus' understanding, the symbolism of the Church functions on several different levels at once. Thus the whole universe, sensible and intelligible, may be seen as a unified organism which has the Church at its heart, while the Church is at the same time an image of this organism, for the same combination of unity and distinction is to be found in both. The Church is primarily an image of the Creator, because of her role in holding together and unifying the cosmos; and then, because she is an image, she represents the whole world in a symbolic and figurative way. The presence of the Church in the world means the presence of God: it means that there is no part of intelligible or sensible creation from which the divine energy is absent, as the cohesive and productive force of the whole universe. The entire sensible and intelligible creation makes up an exquisite temple in which praise and glory are rendered to the Creator.[44] Rational beings alone are capable of interrupting their personal, and therefore free, relaitonship of offering to God and causing the divine energy to absent itself from them, when they make the rest of creation autonomous and distance it from God.

---

43 *Mystagogy*, PG 91.672B.
44 "Things invisible hymn Thee, things visible worship Thee, all performing Thy word, O Master" (Liturgy of St Gregory the Theologian).

Man and the world are not understood as two self-existent, iso-lated, or objective realities. The world cannot exist—at least accord-ing to its nature—once it is placed in a state of apostasy and autonomy from the Church. This is why man, from his very struc-ture and creation, has the charism of being a priest who brings cre-ation into communion with the Holy Trinity when it falls away from that communion and ceases to function as Church. The potential for the world to be churched reveals the dynamic quality of God's cre-ation. God does not despise His creatures. He honors even the small-est component of the world and makes it participate in the mystery of creation. Put to use in this way, the dynamism with which God has bestowed on the world from the beginning is turned to account, and nature's proper mode of functioning is manifested.

After the Fall of man, however, the world too was alienated by the power of evil, which it received. This is why it is man's task to graft the world into the Church, a task which weighs upon him alongside a ceaseless effort of asceticism, repentance, and sanctification. But it is impossible for the world to be taken up and given a place with man in the Church when man's senses are looking for pleasure in his use of the world. Just as one cannot see things except in the light, so we cannot discern the creative dynamism which moves and develops the world and which has its foundation in the uncreated creative energies of God, except with an eye, an intellect, and a consciousness illuminated by the same uncreated energies. Thus it becomes clear why the priority for St Symeon the New Theologian is for man him-self to become part of the Church in reality and truly to repent, with an awareness of his sinfulness.[45] Once man helps himself through the renewing power of repentance, it is easy to remake the rest of cre-ation in the proper way and bring it into the Church. The renewal of persons which precedes the renewal of the world is again accomplished in the Church. Through the Mysteries and

45 *Catechetical Orations* 7, SC 104, p. 54: "For how will someone accept to be healed, if he is not at all convinced that he is suffering from sickness or error?"

services of the Church, and also by studying the Lives of the Saints that offer examples of renewal appropriate to each person, the believer is helped in the spiritual struggle for his own renewal and the churching of his environment.[46]

The churching of the world is to be understood as a gathering of all things that exist into one unity, so that none of them is in opposition or conflict or at enmity with any other, and so as to secure the one nature of sensible things and the "one nature of things created."[47] In this case, man freely participates and becomes a co-worker in the unifying work of God's energies. This cooperation in the unity of beings is manifested in the mysteries of the Church, which are the means whereby rational beings are led up and brought together into the unity of things sensible and intelligible in relation to their unity with the uncreated God.

St Symeon the New Theologian stresses that the mysteries that man is vouchsafed to see by means of the created world are visible, but not comprehensible. Partaking in the mysteries of the Church, the saints and deified Christians receive from the Holy Spirit, the "renewer," all that is required for them to see "sensible things spiritually, and as an image of the invisible."[48] But he does not hesitate to underline that while man is united with Christ in intellect and spirit, at the same time he has the possibility of being united with Him "sensibly and substantially." This "sensible"

---

46 *Catechetical Orations* 5, SC 96, pp. 422-6: "Do you not hear them saying as they read in church, 'Life of St Pelagia, who once was a harlot,' 'Life of St Mary of Egypt, who once was a profligate,' '...of Theodora the adulteress, later a wonder-worker'...?"

47 Maximus the Confessor, *To Thalassius*, Question 48 (PG 90.436B): "And he unified earth and heaven, showing that there is one nature of sensible things, inclining towards itself. And he unified things sensible and things intelligible and showed that there is one nature of things created, joined according to some mysterious inner principle. And according to a principle above nature, he unified created nature with the uncreated." Cf. Dionysius the Areopagite, *On the Heavenly Hierarchy*, PG 3.121D-124A.

48 *Catechetical Orations* 14, SC 104, pp. 212-214.

union is achieved through the mysteries of the Church.[49] Thus the salvation of man as well as the churching of creation is accomplished through the mysteries. The validity and efficacy of the mysteries does not depend on the holiness of the clergy, the general calibre of whom—and of the bishops in particular—was distressingly low in Symeon's time.[50]

The Church has remained positive and receptive in her relationship with matter and world. The Incarnation of God the Word, His entry into history and His assumption of the created, the material, and the temporal, remain the criterion and also the measure for the Church's attitude towards matter and the things of the world. Through the practice and life of the Church, nature is baptized by man into the grace of God, and the corruptible world "puts on incorruption."[51] The churching of the world, its offering back to God, and man's participation in matter sanctified by divine grace—these sum up the "uniformity" of the created beings which these processes graft into the life of the trinitarian God. St Symeon the New Theologian says that this seal of God's grace makes man invulnerable to the darts of the devil and fearless in the face of death. The act of "putting on Christ" in holy Baptism and the "recall" of the Christian in the mystery of penitence give his life its proper orientation in its relationship with God and the world.[52] Through baptism, man participates in the renewal of creation brought about through the Incarnation of Christ. Hence Symeon underlines the significance of this regeneration and the exceptional potential of Christians compared with the righteous and holy people before Christ.[53]

49   *Hymns* 30, SC 174, p. 372.
50   See *Hymns* 58, SC 196, pp. 282-8, lines 64-144.
51   1 Cor 15:54.
52   *Catechetical Orations* 2, SC 96, pp. 252-4.
53   *Catechetical Orations* 5, SC 96, pp. 412-4. Cf. *Chapters* 1.36, SC 51, p. 60, where he stresses characteristically that "baptism has the water that foreshadows tears, and it has the chrism that signifies beforehand the intelligible chrism of the Spirit."

It is especially impressive that man renewed in Christ is not characterized in Scripture as an individual-centered creature, but is seen in the context of the "new creation."[54] In other words, in this state man constitutes a person, who represents in his person the whole world and becomes the cause of the churching of all created things and of creation as a whole. The distinction that contrasts man and creation, which lies at the root of the present ecological crisis, is unknown in the patristic tradition. Man progresses towards renewal and ultimate salvation through and with creation. The "new" man "created according to God" is a "new creation" because he lives in the body of Christ which is the Church. It is only when it is grafted into the Church that the rest of creation too is renewed, as it too awaits its future glory. Only in the Church is the unity and also the deliverance of the whole creation brought about. The redeeming role of the Church for man and the whole of creation is prefigured even from the Old Testament. In an extended typological interpretation, St Symeon the New Theologian underlines that the earthly paradise was a type of the heavenly Jerusalem, the tree of eternal life, which is God.[55] So when man lives in the Church, he feels the need to brings the rest of created things to her and to join them to her as well. In this way he churches the whole creation and becomes the cause whereby it too is brought back to "its ancient and original glory."

The churching of creation with man demonstrates unequivocally that the ontological unity of God and man, established by Christ and cultivated by the Church through her mysteries, presupposes the material and sensible element. Christ and the Church take up the material and sensible and give it its true perspective, the aim of which is not to transcend the sensible but to affirm its worth. This happens when it is sanctified, with a view to the harmonious and universal offering of the spiritual and the

54 2 Cor. 5:17: "if any one is in Christ, he is a new creation." See also Gal 6:15.
55 *Ethical Discourses* 2.3, SC 122, p. 346; *On the Mystical Life*, vol. 1, p. 98.

sensible to God. St Symeon stresses that this taking up and churching of the sensible and material element is realized principally in the mystery of the Divine Eucharist, in which the "ungraspable" God exists "in a body that can be grasped" and the "wholly intangible" and invisible Creator of all becomes "sensible and tangible and visible."[56] The Church as the mystical body of Christ is at once a sensible and a spiritual reality. When she calls man to communion and union with God and exhorts him to lead the rest of material creation to this point and bring it as a eucharistic offering, then far from overlooking his psychosomatic structure, she is approaching him and deifying him in a way proper to his nature.

Elements and good things of the material creation essential for man's life, once they enter the realm of the Church and are used by her, become elements and means of salvation. Water becomes a means of bodily and spiritual purification when we are submerged in it in holy Baptism. Bread and wine, representative elements of material nature, become the Body and Blood of the incarnate Word of God, the Creator and Maker, while oil becomes chrism and a means of healing. This churching and sanctification of matter, the intense symbolic-actual use of matter found in Orthodoxy, can lead to a profound respect for nature. When correctly understood, the sacramental-symbolic life of the Church—of which more is said below—does not present a mere use of matter, but ceaselessly testifies to the intimate existential relationship between God, man, and nature in an unbreakable bond, and also to the interdependence of material and spiritual life. Thus we see a two-way movement: on man's part we have nature and matter brought to the Church as a eucharistic offering; while at the same time matter is taken up by the Creator Himself

---

56 "The ungraspable one is in a body that can be grasped,
    and tangible, and visible, and yet wholly intangible.
    And I, the wretch, do not discern that in those You wish
    You are present in the sensible and tangible and visible
    —the Creator, sensible and tangible and visible."

as a creation continuously being renewed through the energies of the Holy Spirit, so as to become the supreme locus and the means for effecting the communion of God and man.

This is why St Symeon presents the Church as "the world at the height of its loveliness" in which God Himself "dwells and walks," while man receives the rays of His gifts of grace.[57] When the world is churched, it is beautified and becomes wholly church, while the Church becomes identical with the world. In reference to the interpretation of Ps 44:15-16,[58] he underlines that Christ and the Church are inseparably linked concepts. For "just as Christ is head of the Church, and God, so He becomes Himself her temple too, and in turn the Church is established as herself His temple and His world at the height of its loveliness."[59] The Church comes to form the "world in its loveliness" and the "new creation" in replacement of that creation which man lost at the Fall. So when man brings material creation to the Church as an offering, he gives it the possibility of becoming a "world in its loveliness" which will "put man at ease" and give glory to God.

On the other hand, the sanctification by the Church of the material elements and of the entire world has the aim of liberating it from demonic forces. The presence of demons and demonic activities in nature is not rejected, but is given an ecclesial interpretation. Certain services, such as the Blessing of Waters, have a developed demonology. The evil from which man asks to be protected results from the fact that the world "groans" under the power of the devil and is in bondage to vanity and corruption. For

---

57 *Ethical Discourses* 1.7, SC 122, p. 236; *On the Mystical Life,* vol. 1, p. 49: "It seems to me that the world at the height of its loveliness is the Church of Christ, and indeed the whole man himself, in whom God is said to dwell and walk, and upon whom God, the Sun of Righteousness, sends down the bright rays of His charisms." [Translation adapted]

58 Ps 45:14-15 according to the Hebrew numbering: "Virgins shall be brought up behind her and led to the King... they shall be led to the temple of the King."

59 *Ethical Discourses* 1.7, SC 122, p. 238; *On the Mystical Life,* vol. 1, p. 49.

the Church, the demonic reality is not a myth. This is why the churching and sanctification of the material elements (e.g. water) and of nature as a whole has precisely this purpose: to liberate nature from demonic control.[60]

Seeing man's relationship with the world as a purely ecclesial reality, St Symeon stresses that it is essential that our participation in the good things of the world should pass through obedience to a spiritual father.[61] This, of course, presupposes mortification of one's own will—a mortification which, however, brings about man's true and eternal life.[62] In saying "an ecclesial reality," we do not, of course, mean a mere rite cut off from the everyday life of the believer. For within the Church, one cannot see material goods as consumer items, but as things made, products of the love of God. Through true and substantive communion with the other members of the body of Christ, the Church, and through his interpenetration with them, the Christian is called—through his whole way of living, not just through formal participation in the sacraments—to transfigure the things of the world into events of personal relationship and communion, always extending into his daily life the reality of the Church as brotherhood in Christ.

At this point, we should note that a misguided religious education has led many people to regard the Church as a means or instrument for securing their individual salvation. Hence, when they talk abut "salvation," they mean a vague sort of survival after death, usually decked out with plenty of individualistic happiness. In reality, however, the Church lays upon each human being the immense honor and also responsibility of saving the whole

---

60 It is a clear teaching of the Church that the Son of God "appeared to destroy the works of the devil" (1 Jn 3:8). See also Protopresbyter Georgios Metallinos, "Ecological Correspondences," p. 502.

61 *Chapters* 1, 25-28, SC 51, p. 54.

62 *Hymns* 55, SC 196, p. 260:
    "For one who has no will of his own certainly dies,
    but he is in My will, and hence he lives."

world, whose flesh is our flesh and whose life is our life. "Salvation" for the Church means that man lives safe and whole in a universe which is safe and whole. In other words, it is the liberation of life from corruption and death, the transformation of survival into fullness of life, and the participation of the creature in the mode of existence of the uncreated. This is the reason why the Church in the tradition of the Fathers, which is her authentic expression, is not isolated from life and does not look at man independently of the environment and his natural surroundings. On the other hand, it has rightly been pointed out that some contemporary theologians are rather weak on stressing as they should that the salvation of man, which is a purely ecclesial event, is indissolubly related to the salvation and churching of the world, and also to its dynamic progress towards a consummation and perfection. This is why the impression is frequently created that salvation and deification are independent of creation and of life in history as a whole.[63]

Yet in her worship, too—hardly a negligible aspect of her life—the Church has included special services and prayers referring to creation and the life of the faithful in it. These are collected in the *Euchologion* or *Trebnik*, the service book most closely linked with our everyday lives. Apart from the blessing of waters—especially the Great Blessing, which is an incomparable text of Orthodox cosmology—we also find here a host of prayers which embrace the whole of man's life and give him the proper orientation in relating to the natural environment.[64] These are

63 See Paulos Mar Gregorios, *The Human Presence. An Orthodox View of Nature* (Geneva, 1978), pp. 80-81.

64 Just as an example, one could mention the prayers to be read: "for a vessel that has been defiled," "for seed," "for salt," "for the threshing-floor," "at the planting of a vineyard," "for the grape harvest," "for the blessing of wine," "at the building of a boat," "for the blessing of fishing nets," "at the digging of a well," "in time of drought and change of winds," "in time of plague and famine," "for the blessing of a flock," "for silk," "at the inauguration of irrigation works," "at the launching of a boat," etc. See also St Basil, *Homily on Theophany*, PG 31.432Dff., where he speaks at length about the churching and renewal of creation.

prayers which talk about creation, always in relation to man, and look to its sanctification so that it may becomes man's helper and ally in his daily needs. In this way, however, man too is sanctified, since his bond with creation is properly founded, and emphasis is placed on the necessity for harmonious coexistence with it, with the prospect of eschatological salvation. Again, when man sanctifies creation within the Church, he is correspondingly sanctified by it, since in many instances the Church uses it as a means to sanctification and an instrument by which divine grace is conveyed to him.

This testifies to the tremendous creative dynamism that God has bestowed on man and the world—a dynamism which even today could be the starting point for rescuing contemporary creations more generally from corruption. This cannot be accomplished except by grafting into the Church the created things of the world—by churching them, by transfiguring them into the body of Christ, which is the only incorruptible, infinite, and eternal element in our world. With this same movement of grafting, the Church has the capacity to extend as a living reality into every period of history, and Christ can be revealed as the incarnate Word of God and Savior of our world. An excellent example of the churching of created things is afforded by the Fathers; and because of this, they saved these things. They wove the dogmas, the Creed, and the Church's life of worship, using the material of the philosophical, scientific, social and other realities of their day as a weft, but always using as the truth of God's revelation as the warp; and their achievement was to raise this material and the human life built on it to an exalted level above time and death. This effort on their part was so responsible that it did not confine them to somehow retrenching or merely preserving their faith, but spurred them to the hard work and constant struggle necessary for their faith to transform and save the world.[65]

65 See further Nellas, "Christians in the World," pp. 17f.

3. Matter in the Divine Eucharist

The position of Orthodox theology and of the Orthodox Church towards matter is one of affirmation. Orthodox has no connection with any dualism between spirit and matter, soul and body. The whole man is taken up into the Church and his whole life—together with the material needs of his daily life—is related back and offered up to God who "fills all things in Christ" (Eph 4:10). Thus Orthodoxy remains in practice a stranger to any spiritualism, ethereal mysticism, or idealism. It has a direct relation and interest in man's material needs and problems, without however making any of these into an absolute. For the Church, there is no acrimony or opposition between matter and spirit, but everything is seen through the prism of the unity of the sensible and intelligible worlds. Here all creation, things sensible and things intelligible, are united and adorned with the grace of the incarnate God who holds together all creation and "has 'empersoned' in Himself all things, both visible and invisible," since everything within the Church is "visible images of what is hidden, projected; images multiplied and divided of things unique and indivisible; multiform images, with shape, of things that have no form or shape."[66] Only with this yardstick, which Orthodox theology provides and which the Church lives, is materialism able to rid itself of its hostility towards the spiritual aspect of things. With the same yardstick, idealism too is able to rid itself of its unthinkingly belligerent attitude towards matter. With the nourishment that he takes from nature, man lives, puts the world into his body, and changes it into flesh and blood.

In the Church, nothing is only spiritual, because everything presupposes the participation of the human body.[67] But the

---

66 Areopagitic Writings, *Letter* 9.1, PG 3.1105b.

67 On this point, especially characteristic are the words of St John of Damascus addressed to the iconoclasts: "If you would say that we ought to be joined to God in a purely abstract way, then take away everything that is bodily: lights, fragrant

strongest argument against any one-sided approach to spiritual life is that the most real and spiritual relationship between man and God is effected in the Church through the material and sensible Body and Blood of Christ,[68] which are offered to the faithful in Holy Communion and make them partakers in the life of God. The bread and wine, as elements representative of material nature, become the Body and Blood of the incarnate Word of God, the Creator of all. Thus the gifts of the human world come to the Holy Table, to be made incorruptible by an act of grace and changed into the Lord's Body and Blood, the Divine Eucharist. In this way, man is called to become the celebrant of nature with an energy and impetus which is eucharistic and directed back towards God. He offers matter to God in thanksgiving and praise, in order for it to be changed by the Holy Spirit and the Grace of God into the Body and Blood of Christ.

When man approaches and uses the good things of creation in a eucharistic way, then the sensible world—the temple of Christ's presence and place of His praise—becomes in his hands a thank-offering to the Creator. Thus man, who received the world as a divine gift from the hands of the Creator, returns it to God as a gift of his eucharistic thanksgiving. This is perfectly expressed in the priest's exclamation just before the consecration of the Holy Gifts in the Divine Liturgy: "Thine own of Thine own we offer Thee." And this is why the people who make up the eucharistic community then continue: "We praise Thee, we bless Thee, we give thanks to Thee." When man lives eucharistically and liturgically, he receives the world from God as a gift and returns it as thanksgiving, as Eucharist.[69]

incense; even prayer using the voice; even the divine Mysteries performed with matter, the bread, the wine, the oil of anointing, the image of the Cross. For all these things are matter," *On the Divine Images* 1, PG 94.1264AB.

68 *Ibid.*

69 See Hieromonk Gregorios, "The world as liturgical place," 24.

This eucharistic aspect of our vision, our approach and our use of the world, is also stressed by St Symeon the New Theologian. The stage, the image and the expression of how man functions liturgically and relates to the world, is the mystery of the Divine Eucharist, where man the celebrant is vouchsafed such great glory that he celebrates the mystery and sees the unapproachable nature of God.[70] In the Divine Eucharist, the world is made into a personal word-manifestation of God; a word which man receives and dynamically recapitulates in order to offer it back to God from whom it comes forth and to whom it ultimately refers. This is why St Symeon likens those who deny the materiality of the eucharistic bread or—much more—"the deity concealed within it" to the Jews who protested and murmured against Christ when He said that He is "the bread which came down from heaven."[71]

The Eucharist is the sacrament of God's love and His economy towards humans. It is a reiteration of God's economy—which was made manifest with the Incarnation of the Son and Word of God—for the salvation of man and the world. The Holy Spirit sanctifies matter, the bread and the wine, filling it with the grace of God and changing it into the Body and Blood of Christ. The Eucharist becomes the means whereby God's redemptive and transfiguring activity is continued in time. As man eats the flesh of Christ, he becomes one body with Him and wholly His kin "in truth," and "receives of the fullness of His Godhead, and grace upon grace."[72] This "material" communion and relationship gives man the possibility of renewal and causes him to be made incorruptible and sanctified, since by grace he becomes like the God

70 *Hymns* 19, SC 174, p. 98:
  "What man...
  could conceive of anything still more glorious
  than to celebrate the Liturgy and to see the supreme nature
  accomplishing all things, inexpressible, unapproachable to all?"

71 *Ethical Discourses* 3, SC 122, p. 422; *On the Mystical Life*, vol. 1, p. 131. Cf. Jn 6:41-42.

72 *Ethical Discourses* 1.3, SC 122, p. 202; *On the Mystical Life*, vol. 1, p. 33-4. Cf. Jn 1:16.

and Master who loves mankind.[73] In the Divine Eucharist, the unapproachable and ineffable God is seen and eaten by human beings. While he lives this relationship, St Symeon stands amazed at the reality of the eucharistic mystery. This amazement is expressed several times in his hymns, and especially in the following lines:

> How does He deign to see me, and be seen by me,
> and to be held within my hands, who holds the whole universe?[74]

Hence in another hymn he gives thanks and glory to God, not only because he sees Him talking to him and feeding him, but also because God has accounted him worthy "in full reality" to hold and eat His holy Flesh and to drink His all-holy Blood.[75]

The tangible food and drink at the Divine Eucharist corresponds to the psychosomatic unity of the human person. Using material elements, it makes the Body and Blood of the Lord tangible in order to sanctify and deify man in a manner appropriate to his nature. We have already seen how St Symeon expresses this. God's economy, he says, offers man the Body and Blood of Christ in the Divine Eucharist in such a way that the "ungraspable" God exists "in a body that can be grasped" and the "wholly intangible" and invisible Creator of all becomes "sensible and tangible and visible."[76] Man is united with God not in intellect and spirit only, but sensibly as well. The "sensible" relation and union with God is the sacramental union accomplished in Holy Communion.[77] Here it is appropriate to

---

73 *Ibid.*
74 *Hymns* 19, SC 174, p. 96.
75 *Hymns* 20, SC 174, p. 114:
    ... Creator of all, its Maker and Master,
    not only do You see and speak to me, and feed,
    but You have also vouchsafed me, in full reality,
    to hold and eat Your flesh
    and to drink Your all-holy blood."
76 *Hymns* 26, SC 174, p. 272.
77 *Hymns* 30, SC 174, p. 372.

quote also the words of St John of Damascus, which indeed are concerned directly with the subject of icons, but which indirectly underline the value for man of material and sensible communion and relationship with God. Refuting the false anthropology of the iconoclasts, he says with characteristic biting irony: "You, as it happens, are lofty and immaterial; you are above the body, and like one disincarnate, you spit on everything visible. But I, because I am human and clad in a body, long to consort with holy things and see them visibly."[78]

Through his eucharistic use and offering of the world, man cooperates in manifesting the beauty of the earth as a continuously operative blessing of God, which he receives through a personal relationship and communication with Him, namely the mystery of the Eucharist. In the context of this communication, man becomes capable of making the whole earth into a paradise of God's presence. Thus in the ecclesial-eucharistic realm, we succeed in overcoming the division between paradise and the world—thus dealing with at least the fourth of the five oppositions which, according to St Maximus the Confessor, man has to transcend in order to fulfil his natural destiny.[79] For with the Eucharist, another transformion is accomplished, in which creation is transformed. The prospect of a transformed, transfigured world gives a unique dynamic to the history of the world. It is a knowledge unknown to "those that do not believe," and yet stored up as faith and hope in the heart of the Church. At every Divine Liturgy, the eucharistic change of the bread and wine into Body and Blood of Christ is both the firstfruits and the goal of the ultimate transfiguration and renewal of the world. With this prospect and this reality before him, the Christian is not left to be crushed by the steamroller of misuse, and not encage himself in

78 *On the Divine Images* 1, PG 94.1264C.
79 *On Various Difficulties*, PG 91. 1304Dff.; an English translation appears in Nellas, *Deification in Christ*, p. 211ff. See also Lars Thunberg, *Microcosm and Mediator* (Lund, 1965), pp. 147ff.

the bonds of consumerism. He seeks material goods in order to secure his biological existence, but he also has a "mystagogical" attitude which discerns within material things the uncreated Grace, thus making his use of material things into Liturgy and Eucharist.

Referring to this eucharistic dimension, St Symeon the New Theologian makes a parallel between the natural union of the Son and the Father, and the union of Christ and the faithful in the Divine Eucharist. He emphasizes that through things visible and material, Christ leads us up to the invisible glory of "the divinity in His person."[80] The eating of the Divine Eucharist brings about the spiritual union of the believer with Christ.[81] When man eats the "deified flesh" of Christ the Master, he is made immortal as a partaker in true life[82] and communes with the Trinitarian God in His entirety, who is Trinity and at the same time One, and who becomes

bread and wine, the new rich feast of the faithful,
The perfect banquet, the delight in which we mystically delight.[83]

Evident here is the allusion to that communion which is connected with and accompanied by the vision of God. In another hymn, St Symeon addresses a petition to God asking that the heavenly bread should be his travelling companion at the moment of his death.[84] Here it appears that he is making a certain distinction between the heavenly bread and the benevolent

---

80 *Ethical Discourses* 3, SC 122, p. 426; *On the Mystical Life*, vol. 1, p. 133: "The Son of God cries out plainly that our union with Him through communion is such as the unity and life which He has with the Father. Thus, just as He is united by nature to His own Father and God, so we are united by grace to Him, and live in Him, by eating His flesh and drinking His blood. ...Detaching our minds from visible things, or better, leading us up through them to the invisible glory of the divinity in His person..." Cf. Jn 6:56-57.

81 *Ethical Discourses* 2.7, SC 122, p. 380; *On the Mystical Life*, vol. 1, p. 112.

82 *Hymns* 51, SC 196, p. 194.

83 *Hymns* 45, SC 196, p. 104.

84 *Hymns* 49, SC 196, p. 154.

Redeemer who gives it. In reality, he is distinguishing the two functions of the Word, as they appear also in the Prayer of the Cherubic Hymn at the Divine Liturgy of St John Chrysostom: "For You are the one who offers and is offered, who receives and is distributed, Christ our God."

As the Christian experiences the mystery of the Divine Eucharist, he becomes a guest at the marriage ceremony and the royal banquet where Christ the King fills up with every good thing the perceptions of those who recline at the wedding feast, "Himself being the one who is uniquely eaten and drunk, and every kind of food and drink and sweetness."[85] Through this participation in the supper of the Divine Eucharist, Christians feel themselves to be brothers, united among themselves, forming one great family. Indeed, it is this experience that produced the Christians' consciousness of being the one body of Christ, which is the Church.[86] Thus the eucharistic use of the world, which is experienced in the mystery of the Divine Eucharist and in which asceticism is a practical study, becomes a total way of life for every eucharistic community and galvanizes the wider social whole into expressing it in a human culture; a culture such as that which flowered in the so-called Byzantine and post-Byzantine period of Greek history and sprang from precisely the same ecclesial-eucharistic premises.[87]

In order, however, for the Divine Eucharist to become a total way of existence and life, it is necessary for attendance and participation in this mystery to be real. St Symeon declares characteristically that for those who regard participation in the Eucharist as a

---

85 *Ethical Discourses* 3, SC 122, p. 414; *On the Mystical Life*, vol. 1, p. 128.

86 For more detail on this subject see Metropolitan John (Zizioulas) of Pergamon, *The Unity of the Church in the Divine Eucharist and the Bishop during the First Three Centuries* (in Greek) (Athens, 1965), pp. 29-59 (Part I), and G. Mantzaridis, *Sociology of Christianity*, pp. 42-50.

87 On the eucharistic premises of Byzantine civilization see A. Keselopoulos, "The Violation of Creation and the 'Alternative Solution,'" p. 502, and Philip Sherrard, *The Rape of Man and Nature. An Enquiry into the Origins and Consequences of Modern Science* (Suffolk: Golgonooza Press, 1987), pp. 92-94.

formality, the Body and Blood of Christ remain invisible, and consequently "vanish"—as Christ vanished before the eyes of His Disciples after His Resurrection.[88] So the spiritual character of the Divine Eucharist does not permit real participation by those who approach the chalice "without awareness."[89] In the eucharistic gifts Christ Himself is present with His divine and His human nature. In many of his writings, St Symeon insists on the dual character of Divine Communion, the sensible and the spiritual, and stresses that only a conscious communion is true and corresponds to the two natures of Christ.[90] Thus he draws a distinction between the sensible bread and wine and the spiritual gifts, while at the same time drawing a distinction between the Divine Eucharist and the other liturgical acts of the Church.[91] Eucharistic consciousness remains an essential precondition for the efficacy of the mystery.

All the efforts to rescue man's contemporary creations, to discern, evaluate, and take up the objective scientific, technological, and philosophical data of our age and improve the quality of human life in relation to the environment—all these find the possibility of being united and summed up in the Divine Liturgy. It is this that is the "alternative solution" to the problems and blind alleys of contemporary civilization. This is the supreme task of the human community gathered together in peace before the throne of its Creator. The Divine Liturgy, which is first and foremost worship and offering, is also, from the viewpoint that concerns us

88 *Hymns* 26, SC 174, p. 272.

89 *Ethical Discourses* 10, SC 129, p. 314; *On the Mystical Life,* vol. 1, p. 166: "So if we think that all those things take place in us without our knowledge and awareness, who could adequately grieve for our lack of feeling? Truly, no one."

90 Translator's note: Symeon's striking emphasis on the impotance of "conscious awareness" in receiving the Body and Blood of Christ, and the misunderstandings that this has occasioned among those who read him, anachronistically, through post-Reformation spectacles, are lucidly discussed by Fr Alexander Golitzin, *On the Mystical Life,* vol. 3, pp. 111-116.

91 *Ethical Discourses* 14, SC 129, pp. 436-8; *On the Mystical Life,* vol. 1, pp. 179-80.

here, a responsible and decisive reorganization of life on the part of Christians. It transforms time and space, human relationships with each other, and human relationships with creation. Its character as thanksgiving causes Christians to receive life, the fruits of their fellow humans' work, and the whole of nature as gifts— from their fellow human beings, but first and foremost from God. They feel the need to offer these gifts back; for all to offer them to all, and then for all together to offer them to God, with the selflessness and joy that come from receiving and also giving gifts. Certainly this eucharistic character of life is at the opposite pole from the mania for consumption which dominates our contemporary culture. But if this eucharistic quality is presented and lived out and is then projected by Christians into the world, it will be possible to realize the required "Copernican revolution of the mind"[92] and to free our society from its radical functional inadequacies.

92 See D. Meadows, *The Limits to Growth* (New York, 1972), p. 175 (2nd edition, New York, 1989, p. 196).

Summary

In the theology and cosmology of St Symeon, nature is regarded as creation, something made by God. It is presented as the supreme mystery, which has been celebrated by the Trinitarian God not as the shaping of an existing reality or the bestowal of a quality, but as bringing forth and creating out of nothing. This is the fundamental difference between God's creation and man's creations. God's creations have real existence, because as creations out of nothing they are not grounded in themselves—since their nature of itself is mutable and corruptible and has lurking within it a literally ontological annihilation, in other words the non-being out of which they came. Rather, they are grounded in the will of God which is all-powerful, beyond any notion of beginning or end, and absolutely steadfast and full of love. God's creations are real and open to eternity in a manner proper to Him (to a degree far greater than humans can understand), because they exist thanks to God's eternal and unchanging will. By contrast, human creations always come out of some pre-existing matter and are in reality mere constructions. Even the greatest inventions or the most original works of art are nothing more than discoveries, things that have come to light. Man's creations are the result of a created and consequently mutable will, and a created and therefore limited mind. This is why they contain within them mutability and corruption, being orientated towards death. An indisputable example from history is the inevitable death of civilizations. So while the creations of man, when God is not working with him, are subject to time and orientated towards corruption, God's creations are orientated towards life and eternity.

The world exists as the work of the three Persons of God in Trinity. St Symeon exhorts his reader to be led by the things that exist, not only to believe that there is a God who is the cause of creation, but principally to learn and understand the manner in which this God exists. From the order, the harmony, and also the differences that exist among existent things, one learns of the love of God the Father who engenders them, of the personified Wisdom of God, God the Word, who holds them all together, and of the Holy Spirit who is the life-giving force in them. From the apophatic approach to the universe, one learns the apophatic knowledge and understanding of God. The One and Trinitarian God brings forth the whole world "out of non-being," "gives it being," and "ineffably holds it in existence." His command guards and preserves all things. The Wisdom of the Father exercises providence for all things; He intends the creatures of the world "before all ages" and wills them and loves them. Furthermore, the true beauty of the world reveals this very providence, will, and love of the Father. But this revelation is *logos*, a "word". It is the manifestation of the Energy of the Son and Word "through whom all things were made." The One that "brings down" and "creates" and "brings forth all things by the Word," holds all these things together by the lifegiving power of the Holy Spirit.

The entire creation is in a direct relationship to God and forms a realm of his presence. But the relationship between God and the world at the same time presupposes otherness and radical difference. Again, this stems from the truth that the world is created out of nothing. God, being uncircumscribed by essence and nature, is both within the world and outside it. On the other hand, all created things are within God inasmuch as He "creates and holds together all things," but at the same time they are outside God because things created are separated from the uncreated God. The existence of God as cause of all things, Creator and Maker of all that is created, explains the simultaneous distance of God from all that He has made. Furthermore, God is and exists as love; love is an "all-creating light" which lightens all created things and all the world, without coming from the world or having anything in common with any created thing of this world.

The realm of worldly reality is a place of God, since from created things the Maker of them is known. The beauty of created things leads man up to God, the author of existence, and exhorts man to a relationship of praise with the Maker of all things. Yet in order for the world to be revealed to man as a dimensionless *locus* of the divine personal Energy, man needs to remain "within his own limits." Only thus can he achieve the self-transcendence of his own individuality that makes possible the experiential approach to the personal existence of God. In the framework of man's personal relationship with the Creator of all—a relationship whose hallmark is faith—the world is no longer given a conventional autonomy as a neutralized object whose only value lies in its usefulness. In this case the world "contains," "gives space," for God's relationship with man. A person who has the mind of Christ and desires to know the exterior beauty of created things discovers the approachability of God through the reality of the creation of the world, without this removing God's natural distance from the world, which is the distance of uncreated nature from created. So in this way it is possible for man "from created things proportionately to wonder at the origin of their being"; but he cannot confuse uncreated and created nature or identify creation with the Creator and worship created things while ignoring the Maker. From the greatness and beauty of created things man can have an awareness of the Creator and know Him better. Then he realizes that his closeness to God through the world is not by nature but by place—that is, it is a closeness created by His personal relationship with God. Thus he understands that it is not the world that "contains" God, but the will and Energy of God that "contains" the world. If one does not respect this apophaticism in the relation between created and uncreated—an apophaticism constituted by the interdependence of God and the world and the simultaneous distinction between them—it is very easy to fall into the heresy of idealistic or materialistic humanism, which in the final analysis are two sides of the same coin.

On the other hand man, by reason of his physiology, has a direct relationship and kinship with the rest of creation, since besides his spiritual dimension he also has a material dimension. One of the basic materials he is made of is earth, in other words his physical and biological components. From this point of view, he is a part of the physical creation and a biological being, which in its structure and functioning does not differ much from other physical beings. Materiality, albeit developed to higher forms than in plants and animals, is a basic and inalienable element in his being. Furthermore, the unity, cohesion, and common origin of creation testifies to the unified and dynamic character in the relationship between cosmology and anthropology. The one world cannot be examined without reference to the other, nor can either of the two elements of creation be looked at in isolation and independently from its relationship to the other. All the levels of existence associated with the various forms in the created world are to be found in man. This again is why the physiology of man, as it is presented in the writings of St Symeon and other Fathers, bears a direct relation to Orthodox cosmology and is of essential concern to it.

In accordance with the physiology of man and his creation in the image of God, it is maintained that he is an indissoluble unity of spirit and body, and stress is laid on the indwelling of the uncreated in the created, which is the greatest honor and affirmation of the human body that God bestows. Having been created in the image of the personal God and the personal Word, man forms the created hypostasis of the inner principles of existent things. As a true "microcosm," he sums up all created realities and receives the natural dynamism of creation, which he is called to guide to its end. By virtue of being in God's image, man is called by God to preserve and consummate the proper orientation of this dynamism. He will achieve this task when he makes proper use of the gifts and natural powers with which he has been endowed by being in God's image.

Between the world and man there is a relationship of analogy. The world can be described "on a small scale" in man, while man can be seen "on a large scale" in the world. The soul of the world is the intelligible creation, and its body is the sensible. In man, again, his soul is the intelligible creation and his body the sensible. The world stands as an image and type of what takes place in man. Taking images from the sun, the moon, and other heavenly bodies, St Symeon applies them to man and underlines that the world as an image of man was not invented by humans; it was constructed that way by God Himself. In creation, the craftsman Word of God "sketched in advance" as in a picture what was to take place for the salvation of man. This was so that man should be able to see the image revealed in sensible things, and so not disbelieve that in himself as well, "the real truth is brought to completion" and spiritually accomplished.

The whole of material creation was given by God to man as a blessing and a gift. In an interpretation of the relevant passage in Genesis, St Symeon underlines that God did not give man paradise alone, but the whole of the earth. In his exegesis of the expression "to till and keep it" in the Old Testament, he says that these two verbs represent interrelated concepts which refer both to man's rights and to his responsibilities towards the environment in which he lives. A right use of creation, i.e. the "tilling," necessarily implies also a duty of further protecting and conserving creation, the "keeping." Right use of creation without at the same time protecting it is not possible. Man is called to "till" in a responsible manner as God's representative and steward, but also as the overseer and guard of the natural world. On the other hand, the command to "subdue the earth" does not constitute man's passport to irresponsible and unrestrained maltreatment and destruction of the natural environment. If man was especially honored by God in comparison with all other creatures and hence "rules and reigns over them," this does not mean that his relationship to the environment can be that of an oppressor to his victim. Man's sovereignty over nature brings with it corresponding responsibilities, because it is an accountable authority. Furthermore, the meaning of man's dominion in creation is not unconditional. It belongs in the context of his ability to use the potentialities of creation aright so that it helps and serves him. The ultimate problem in the relations between man and creation is not who will dominate whom, but how man can live in harmony with the other creatures of God.

In the relationship between man and creation, it is not creation that brings man to God, but man who ultimately "makes creation word." This task has its starting point in man's natural potential for mediation between God and the world and is consummated when man is deified and creation is brought back to the beauty in which it was first created—that is, with the complete interpenetration of created and uncreated. It is the task which Adam failed to accomplish because of the Fall. Thus man himself disrupts the harmony of his relations with creation, since by the Fall and his disobedience to God's command he also alters his conduct towards the rest of creation. Furthermore, God's command has a direct relation to the use of the world and of creation (Gen 2:17). Because man did not keep the command and did not behave properly in the place and the environment in which he was put, he took the consequences. But man also bears particular responsibility for the state to which creation is reduced, since it too bore the consequences of man's conduct and was unwillingly made subject to vanity and enslavement. St Symeon the New Theologian particularly underlines that the enslaved state of creation is not part of its natural development. Creation is presented as a victim, because on man's account it loses its proper position and rule of operation. This is why it refuses to submit to man once he has transgressed.

The change and alienation that the earth, and indeed the whole of creation, undergoes after the Fall, shows that its first principle is to be found in God. The violation of creation by man, on the other hand, occurs in the measure that he distances himself from God. Man's transgression of God's commandment, and above all his lack of repentance, was what sent man away from paradise, since in the fallen state his alienation has a direct effect over the whole of creation. This is why the world in its fallen state loses its original meaning as an adornment and a creation of God and becomes charged with a negative significance. There arises a sinful and empassioned relationship with things which is instigated by the prince of this world, the devil, and falls under his influence. Nevertheless God, as Creator and Maker of all, rules all things "by nature and with authority." The devil operates in creation as a parasitic force. Hence the so-called natural world is not at all natural, since it is not in the original state of its creation, but in a state of fallenness and rebellion which leads to corruption and death.

As a consequence of the Fall, we see the tendency to make creation and material goods autonomous, something that cannot under any circumstances be interpreted as a real love for them. When man makes creation and material goods autonomous from their Maker, he is living in an empassioned state. He is subservient to the material world, not because he desires it and loves it in a right way, but because he has perverted his capacity of will and separated it from the life-giving energy of God. Man does not make matter autonomous because he himself has a material component, but because his attitude to it is wrong. When the world is made autonomous and cut off from its cause which is God, it essentially ceases to exist; it is reduced to a state of non-being. Hence St Symeon says that when the world is in this state—essentially, when man adopts this stance towards it—then it does not belong among "things stable" but among "things in flux." This attitude—on which the whole phenomenon of modern technology is clearly founded—regards the world as autonomous, and therefore goes so far as to make it an absolute and a god. On the other hand, when knowledge of the world departs from an Orthodox context which presupposes that the world is always to be looked at through man's relationship with the Creator, it then acquires autonomy and becomes a knowledge with its own structure and organization. It is no longer expressed in the "significative" terminology of aesthetics or theology, but through an objectively articulated scientific method which is able—supposedly—to predict and explain everything that takes place in nature.

From making the world autonomous man goes on to misuse it when, with "usefulness" as the yardstick, the world is turned into an impersonal object and violated unrestrainedly so that it ultimately submits to man's greed and avarice. The Fathers stress that it is on the basis of man's relationship with the things of the world and the way he uses them—depending on whether it is rational or irrational—that he is characterized accordingly as either virtuous or vicious. St Symeon maintains unequivocally that people who do not have a right relationship with the things of the world are as it were outside the world, living a life contrary to nature. Hence it is natural that his cosmology should reject consumption and the acquisition of wealth as forms of misuse of the world. Furthermore, individualistic domination of the world and the mentality of consumerism, as these are served and secured today by technology on the one hand and misguided economic notions on the other, are the practical application of a cosmology poles apart from that of St Symeon and the Fathers—one that sees nature as an impersonal and neutral datum at the service of man's desires and his endless "needs."

The opposite pole from misuse of the world is the eucharistic use of it, which takes as its starting point a study of the inner principles of existent things and respect for these principles. All God's creations have as their foundation and inner structure the "words" of God, which show through these results of God's creative work. St Symeon refs in several of his writings to the inner principles of the beings in creation and underlines the importance of man's discovering and understanding them. Man is led to an increase in faith and a growth in his love for God through a variety of signs, among which is contemplation of the inner principles of creation. One cannot acquire a perfect love for God as an inalienable possession without spiritual knowledge of the inner principle in the created things of the world through which God, their Maker and Creator, is contemplated. Through the inner principle of created things we see in action the harmony of the world, which makes it possible for man to have personal relationships with the world and also with the Creator. Hence the purpose of things and also of man, the "principle of their being" or *raison d'être*, is a fundamental element in St Symeon's theology.

The existence of the world does not guarantee man a true perception of the nature of things and in consequence a genuine encounter with the inner principles of the things in creation. Enslavement to the passions is always a hindrance to this encounter. It is necessary first for man to live true repentance as a change in his way of thinking, in order for him then to be given the possibility of orientating himself rightly towards creation and developing a relationship of love with the things of the world. The inner principles, the "words" of things, have their origin, their substance, and their end in the divine Word who is the source of the rationality of the world. This is precisely why man needs awareness of the presence of the Word of God in order to be able to know and encounter the "words," the inner principles of things.

In order to approach the inner principles of things, it is necessary first to be using the world in accordance with nature; whereas any discord in man's relations with his natural surroundings indicates that something of the unnatural and irrational has infiltrated these relations. But if irrationality and an unnatural state are manifested in misuse of the world, then respect for the inner principles ("rationales") of things and a natural state is expressed in the ascetic, non-consumerist, and eucharistic use of the world. Dominant in the first instance are the hedonistic demands of the senses, which inform man about creation in a manner which does not correspond to the truth of things. In this way they change the beauty of creation and oblige it to submit to the service of human individuality and autonomy. In the second instance, we have a renunciation on man's part of the demands of the senses, which constitutes the ascetic-eucharistic use of the world, the sole way of true life and knowledge. In St Symeon's writings, especial stress is laid on the ascetic use of the world which, in contrast to the consumerist use, saves not only the world but man too. For this reason, "absolute necessity for the body" is held up as the measure and "better way" in use of the world, a way which also works towards social justice.

Especially for the present age of incalculable exploitation and violation of the environment, the ascetic and non-consumerist ethos promoted by the Fathers is particularly salutary, since it shows man the way to restrict his greedy appetites towards creation in order to be connected with it in a more real and harmonious way, as God created him to be. This is the ethos embodied by the charismatic monks (not that they are the only expression of it) who by their life preserve truth, authenticity, and respect in their relations with the nature that surrounds them. Their asceticism is not to be interpreted as abhorrence of matter and the natural environment, but as the transcendence of human individualism. The true monk does not maltreat material things or the environment, but takes care of them and respects them. Thus in the life of the monk and the way he uses things, matter and the environment are elevated to their original beauty.

The task of mediation between God and the world was not fulfilled by the first Adam. But it found its fulfilment in the person of the second Adam, Christ, who became the father of the "new creation." The Incarnation of the Word took place at a time when man had defiled creation not only by using it wrongly, but even by deifying it. With the renewal of man in Christ, the whole of creation is renewed as well. A new creation means a re-creation in dynamic relation to the Creator Word, the Word-Principle of all beings, and so in relation not only to God, but also to nature as His creation. Within Orthodox theology, cosmology and anthropology have a Christological foundation and are looked at through the prism of re-creation in Christ, which is a realization of the mystery of the divine economy for the salvation of man and the transfiguration of the world. Man's relationship with creation has a Christological grounding and a soteriological perspective. Only in this context does it realize its value and acquire content and purpose.

The Church, the body of the incarnate Christ, forms the potentiality for bringing together into one the whole world. If the Church, which is the communion of rational and intelligible beings, did not exist, then creation would not be able to have a relationship of knowledge and conscious participation in the energies of God. The entire universe makes up an organic unity with the Church as its heart. The presence of the Church in the world signifies the presence of God. In consequence, there is no part of intelligible or sensible creation from which the divine energy can be absent as the cohesive and productive force of the entire universe. Thus we have the "churching" of material creation and its participation in the glory of God. The world cannot exist—at least in accordance with nature—in a state of rebellion and autonomy from the Church. Hence man, by his very make-up and creation, has the gift of being the priest who brings creation into communion with the Holy Trinity when it falls away from that communion and ceases to function as Church. Because after the Fall creation was alienated by the power of evil which it received, it is the responsibility of re-created man to graft the world into the Church. Furthermore, the potentiality for churching the world shows the dynamic quality of God's creation.

Finally, the mystery of the Church, the Divine Eucharist—which is man's most essential and spiritual relationship with God—is accomplished through the material and sensible Body and Blood of Christ which is offered to the faithful and makes them partakers in the life of God. The bread and the wine, as the elements representative of material nature, become the Body and Blood of the incarnate Word of God, the Maker of creation. In this way man is called to become the celebrant of nature with an energy and impetus which is eucharistic and leads back to God. This eucharistic dimension to our use of the world is not a mere detail in the writings of the Fathers and St Symeon. It is the most essential element, which could assist towards a different approach, a different view of the relationship between man and the natural environment. It is the 'alternative solution' to the problems and blind alleys of contemporary civilization.

BIBLIOGRAPHY

1. Works of St Symeon

Critical editions of the works of St Symeon are to found in the series Sources chrétiennes (SC), Paris, Editions de Cerf.

Catechetical Discourses: Catéchèses, ed. B. Krivochéine and J. Paramelle.

    I. *Catéchèses* 1-5, SC 96, 1963.
    II. *Catéchèses* 6-22, SC 104, 1964.
    III. *Catéchèses* 23-24, SC 113, 1965.

ET *Symeon the New Theologian: The Discourses*, tr. C.J. deCantanzaro (New York: Paulist Press, 1980).

Chapters: Chapitres théologiques, gnostiques et pratiques, ed. J. Darrouzès, SC 51, 1957.

ET *St Symeon the New Theologian: The Practical and Theological Chapters*, tr. and introd. J. McGuckin (Kalamazoo: Cistercian Studies, 1982).

Ethical Discourses: Traités théologiques et ethiques, ed. J. Darrouzès.

    I. *Théol.* 1-3, *Eth.* 1-3, SC 122, 1966.
    II. *Eth.* 4-15, SC 129, 1967.

ET *St Symeon the New Theologian On the Mystical Life: The Ethical Discourses*, vols. 1 & 2, tr. Alexander Golitzin (Crestwood, 1995, 1996).

Hymns: Hymnes, ed. J. Koder, J. Paramelle and L. Neyrand.

    I. *Hymnes* 1-15, SC 156, 1969.
    II. *Hymnes* 16-40, SC 174, 1971.
    III. *Hymnes* 41-58, SC 196, 1973.

ET *Hymns of Divine Love*, tr. G. Maloney (Denville, New Jersey: Dimension Books, no date).

Letters: Letter 1, On Confession, ed. K. Holl in *Enthusiasmus und Bussgewalt beim griechischen Mönchtum* (Leipzig, 1898), pp. 110-127.

ET in Alexander Golitzin, *St Symeon the New Theologian, On the Mystical Life: The Ethical Discourses; vol. 3:* Life, Times and Theology (Crestwood, 1997), pp. 186-203.

Letters 2-4—unedited. The text appears in codex Coisl. 292, fol. 263-273.

Thanksgiving: Actions de grâces 1 and 2, SC 113, 1965.

Theological Discourses: Traités théologiques et ethiques, ed. J. Darrouzès. I. Théol. 1-3, Eth. 1-3, SC 122, 1966.

2. *Secondary Sources*

Ahrweiler, H., *L'idéologie politique de l'empire byzantin,* Paris 1975.

Allchin, A.M., "Creation, Incarnation, Interpretation." A.M. Allchin (ed.), *Sacrament and Image,* Fellowship of St Alban and St Sergius, London 1967, pp. 42-56 (Second edition, London 1987, pp. 47-63).

Allers, R., "Microcosmos from Anaximandros to Paracelsus." *Traditio* 2 (1944), pp. 319-407.

Armstrong, A.M., "The Theory of the Non-Existence of Matter in Plotinus and the Cappadocians." *Studia Patristica* 5 (1962), pp. 427-429.

Bach, E., "les lois agraires byzantines du Xe siècle." *Classica et Mediaevalia* V (1942), pp. 70-91.

Balthasar, H.U. von, *Liturgie Cosmique: Maxime le Confesseur,* Paris 1947.

Barbour, I.C., *Western Man and Environmental Ethics. Attitudes towards Nature and Technology,* Reading, Mass. 1973.

Black, J., *The Dominion of Man. The Search for Ecological Responsibility,* Edinburgh 1970.

Blackstone, T., *Philosophy and Environmental Crisis,* Athens 1974.

Brehier, *Les institutions de l'empire byzantin,* Paris 1948.

Burckhardt, T., "Cosmology and Modern Science." *Tomorrow* (London), Summer 1964.

Bury, J.B., *The Imperial Administrative System in the Ninth Century,* second edition, New York 1963.

Callahan, J., "Greek Philosophy and the Cappadocian Cosmology." *Dumbarton Oaks Papers* 12 (1958), pp. 31-57.

Charanis, P., "On the Social Structure of the Later Roman Empire." *Byzantion* 17 (1944-45), pp. 38-57.

Chrestou, P.K., "Agios Symeon o Theologos tou Photos." *Synaxi* 10 (1984), 9-16. Clément, O., "Le sens de la terre (notes de cosmologie orthodoxe)." *Contacts* 59-60 (1967), pp. 252-323.

Derr, T.S., *Ecology and Human Need*, The Westminster Press 1975.

Disch, R., *The Ecological Conscience. Values for Survival*, Englewood Cliffs, NJ 1970.

Doikos, D., *O anthropos kata tin Palaian Diathikin*, Thessaloniki 1969.

——— *Synoptiki Eisagogi stin Palaia Diathikin*, Thessaloniki 1980.

Dubarle, D., *Approches d'une théologie de la science*, Paris 1967.

Dvornik, F., *Early Christian and Byzantine Political Philosophy*, Dumbarton Oaks 1966.

Eliade, M., *the Myth of the Eternal Return*, London 1955.

Efthymios (Stylios) (Bishop of Acheloos), *To synchronon astikon perivallon os poimantikon provlima* [*The Modern Urban Environment as a Pastoral Problem*], Athens 1980.

Florovsky, G., "The Idea of Creation in Christian Philosophy." *Eastern Churches Quarterly* 8.3 (1949), pp. 53-77.

——— "The Concept of Creation in St Athanasius." *Studia Patristica* 6 (1962), pp. 36-57.

——— "Eschatology in the Patristic Age: An Introduction." *Studia Patristica* 2 (1957).

Galanis, I., *I schesi anthropou kai ktiseos kata tin Kaini Diathiki* [The Relationship between Man and Creation according to the New Testament], Thessaloniki 1984.

——— "To kainodiathikiko ypovathro ton scheseon anthropou kai ktisis kata ti latreftiki praxi tis Ekklesias" [The New Testament Foundation for the relations between Man and Creation in the Church's Worship]. *Volume in Honor of Professor Emeritus Konstantinos Kalokyris*, pp. 383-400.

Gilson, E., *History of Christian Philosophy in the Middle Ages*, New York 1955.

Gousidis, A., *Ekklesia kai Koinonia* [Church and Society], Thessaloniki 1982.

Gregorios (Hieromonk of the Holy Mountain), *I Leitourgia tis Efcharistias tou Theou*, Monastery of Chalkis, 1971.

——— *I Theia Leitourgia—Scholia*, second edition, Athens 1985.

——— "O kosmos topos leitourgikos" [The World as Liturgical Place]. *Synaxi* 14 (1985), pp. 21-24.

Gregorios, P., *The Human Presence. An Orthodox View of Nature*, Geneva 1978, New York 1987.

Hadjimichalis, N. (now Metropolitan of Leros and Kalymnos), *Ai peri idioktisias apopseis en ti ekklesia kata tous treis protous aiones* [Views on Private Property in the Church during the First Three Centuries], Thessaloniki 1972.

Heisenberg, W., *The Physicist's Conception of Nature* [translation of *Naturbild der heutigen Physik*], New York 1958.

———— *Physics and Philosophy: The Revolution in Modern Science*, New York 1958.

Hussey, J.M., *Church and Learning in the Byzantine Empire*, London 1937.

Isaias (Monk of Simonopetra), "O agios Symeon o Neos Theologos os pnevmatikos odigos." *Synaxi* 10 (1984), pp. 37-42.

Jevtic, Athanasios (Metropolitan), "To perivallon kai to prosopo" [The Environment and the Person,] in *Spoudi ston Dostoevski* [A Study on Dostoevski], Halandri, 1983.

Karavidopoulos, I., *"Eikon Theou" kai "kat' eikona Theou" para to Apostolo Pavlo* ["Image of God" and "in the image" of God in St Paul], Thessaloniki 1964.

Keselopoulos, A., *Pathi kai aretes sti didaskalia tou Agiou Gregoriou tou Palama* [Passions and Virtues in the Teaching of St Gregory Palamas], (first reprint Athens 1986).

———— "O viasmos tis ktisis kai i alli lysi" [The Rape of Creation and the "Alternative Solution"]. Volume of *Diakonia* dedicated to the memory of V. Stoyannos, Thessaloniki 1987, pp. 491-503.

Kolyvas, I.-K., "I orthodoxi prooptiki sto ergo tou Papadiamanti" [The Orthodox Perspective in the Work of Papadiamantis]. *Diavazo* 165, pp. 80-90.

Krivocheine, B. (Archbishop), *In the Light of Christ*, Crestwood 1986.

———— "Le thème de l'ivresse spirituelle dans la mystique de St Syméon le Nouveau Théologien." *Studia Patristica* V (1962), pp. 368-376.

Kyriazopoulos, S., *I katagogi tou technikou pnevmatos* [The Origin of the Technical Spirit], Athens 1965.

———— *I parousia tis physikis epistemis*, Athens 1963.

Lampe, G.W.H., "The New Testament Doctrine of Ktisis." *Scottish Journal of Theology* 19 (1964), pp. 449-462.

Land, P. (ed.), *Theology Meets Progress*, Gregorian University Press 1971.

Leiss, W., *The Domination of Nature*, New York 1972.

Mantzaridis, G., *Palamika*, Thessaloniki 1983.

——— *Christianiki Ethiki* [*Christian Ethics*], second ed., Thessaloniki 1983.

——— *Koinoniologia tou Christianismou* [*Sociology of Christianity*], Thessaloniki 1985.

——— *Orthodoxi Pnevmatiki Zoi* [*Orthodox Spiritual Life*], Thessaloniki 1986.

——— *Eisagogi stin Ethiki. I Ethiki stin krisi tou parontos kai tin proklisi tou mellontos* [*Introduction to Ethics*], Thessaloniki 1988.

Martzelos, G., *Ousia kai Energeia tou Theou kata ton Megan Vasileion*, Thessaloniki 1984.

Mascal, E., *Christian Theology and Natural Science*, London 1956.

Mathew, G.A., *Byzantine Aesthetics*, London 1963.

Matsoukas, N., *Genesis kai ousia tou orthodoxou dogmatos*, Thessaloniki 1969.

——— "Logos kai mythos me vasi tin archaia elliniki philosophia." *Epistimoniki Epeteris tis Theologikis Scholis Thessalonikis* 21 (1976), pp. 187-294.

——— *To provlima tou kakou. Dokimion paterikis theologias* [*The Problem of Evil; An Essay in Patristic Theology*], Thessaloniki 1976.

——— *Kosmos, Anthropos, Koinonia kata ton Maximo Omologiti* [*World, Man and Communion according to Maximus the Confessor*], Athens 1980.

——— "Epistimonika, philosophika kai theologika stoicheia tis Exaemerou tou M. Vasileiou." *Tomos eortios chiliostis exakosiostis epeteiou Megalou Vasileiou (379-1979)*, Thessaloniki 1981, pp. 43-148.

Meadows, D., *The Limits of Growth*, New York 1972, 1989.

Metallinos, G., "Oikologikes antistoichies kai anantistoichies Ellinismou kai Christianismou" [Ecological Correspondences and Discrepancies between Hellenism and Christianity]. *Koinonia* 28.4 (1985), pp. 496-516.

Meyendorff, J., "Orthodox Theology Today." *Sobornost* 6.1 (1970).

——— *Christ in Eastern Christian Thought*, Crestwood, 1987.

Michelis, P.A., *Aisthitiki theorisi tis vyzantinis technis*, second ed., Athens 1972.

Moltmann, J., "Theologische Begründung der Menschenrechte." *Politische Theologie—Politische Ethik*, Munich 1984, 116-179.

Nasr, S.H., *The Encounter of Man and Nature*, London 1968.

Nellas, P., "I theologia tou 'kat' eikona'" [The Theology of God's image in man]. *Kleronomia* 2.II, Thessaloniki 1970, pp. 293-322.

———— "Oi Christianoi mesa ston kosmo" [Christians in the World]. *Synaxi* 13 (1985), pp. 7-25.

———— *Deification in Christ*, Crestwood 1987.

———— "Oi Christianoi mesa ston kosmo" [Christians in the World]. *Synaxi* 13 (1985), p. 10.

Nilsson, M., *Elliniki Laiki Thriskeia* [*Greek Folk Religion*] (tr. I. Th. Kakridis), Athens 1979.

Nikodimos of the Holy Mountain, *Asmatiki Akolouthia tou en Agiois Patros Imon Symeon tou Neou Theologou*, Syros 1777.

Nissiotis, N., *Prolegomena eis tin theologikin gnoseologian* [*Prolegomena to Theological Gnoseology*], Athens 1965.

———— "I physi os ktisi" [Nature as creation]. *Synaxi* 14 (1985), pp. 11-20.

Oikonomou, I., *Theologiki theorisis ton provlimaton tou perivallontos*, Athens 1973.

Orphanos, M., *Creation and Salvation according to St Basil of Caesarea*, Athens 1975.

Papathanasiou, Th., "O anachoritismos—Metamorphosi tis erimou se topo despoteias tou Theou" [The Anchoretic Life—Transforming the Desert into a Place of God's Dominion]. *Synaxi* 13 (1985), pp. 38-40.

Petrou, I., *Koinoniki dikaiosyni* [*Social Justice*], Thessaloniki 1986.

Prestige, G.L., *God in Patristic Thought*, London 1952.

Reclam, P., *Ökologie und Ethik*, Stüttgart 1980.

Rossum, J. van, *The Ecclesiological Problem in St Symeon the New Theologian*, New York 1976.

———— "Priesthood and Confession in St Symeon the New Theologian." St Vladimir's Seminary Quarterly 20 (1976), pp. 220-228.

Roszak, T., *Where the Wasteland Ends*, London 1973.

Samuel, P., *Ecologie: détente ou cycle infernal*, Paris 1973.

Sherrard, P., "The Art of the Icon," in A.M. Allchin (ed.), *Sacrament and Image*, second edition, London 1987, pp. 64-76.

———— *The Rape of Man and Nature. An Enquiry into the Origins and Consequences of Modern Science*, Ipswich 1987.

Sophrony (Archimandrite), *St Silouan the Athonite*, Tolleshunt Knights 1991 / Crestwood 1999.

Staniloae, D., "Phos Christou phainei pasi" [The Light of Christ Shines upon All], reprint from *Epistimoniki Epeteris tis Theologikis Scholis Thessalonikis*, Thessaloniki 1976.

———— "The World as Gift and Sacrament of God's Love." *Sobornost* 5:9 (1969), pp. 662-673.

———— "I mystiki empeiria ston agio Symeon kai ston M. Eckart" [Mystical experience in St Symeon and in Meister Eckart]. *Synaxi* 10 (1984), pp. 27-35.

———— *Sto phos tou Stavrou kai tis Anastaseos* [In the light of the Cross and the Resurrection], Monastery of the Transfiguration, Kymi 1984.

Stone, G.C., *A New Ethics for a New Earth*, New York 1971.

Theodorou, A., *Soteriologiki ermineia tis theias Metamorphoseos tou Soteros* [A soteriological interpretation of the Transfiguration of the Saviour], Athens 1968.

Theoklitos (Monk of Dionysiou), "Pnevmatiki zoi kai theologia kata ton Symeon ton Neo Theologo" [Spiritual life and theology according to Symeon the New Theologian]. *Synaxi* 10 (1984), pp. 17-26.

Thunberg, L., *Microcosm and Mediator: The Theological Anthropology of Maximus the Confessor*, Lund 1965.

Toynbee, A., *Constantine Porphyrogenitus and his World*, second edition, Oxford 1973.

Tsamis, D., *I protologia tou M. Vasileiou*, Thessaloniki 1970.

———— *Anthropos kai perivallon sti skepsi ton Trion Ierarchon* [Man and the Environment in the Thought of the Three Hierarchs], Thessaloniki 1977.

———— *Eisagogi stin Pateriki Skepsi* [*Introduction to Patristic Thought*], Thessaloniki 1985.

Tselengidis, D., *I theologia tis eikonas kai i anthropologiki simasia tis* [The theology of the Icon and its Anthropological Significance], Thessaloniki 1984.

Vasileiadis, P.B., *Charis, Koinonia, Diakonia: O Koinonikos Charactiras tou Pavleiou Programmatos tis Logeias*, Thessaloniki 1985.

Vasileios (Archimandrite), *Hymn of Entry*, Crestwood 1984.

———— "Apo ton Palaio sto Neo Adam." *Synaxi* 2 (1982), pp. 21-30.

———— *Theologiko scholio stis toichographies tis Ieras Monis Stavronikita* [Theological Commentary on the Frescoes of the Holy Monastery of Stavronikita], Athens 1987 (Reprinted from Manolis Hadjidakis (ed.), *O Kritikos zographos Theophanis* [The Cretan Painter Theophanes], Holy Mountain 1986.

Ware, Kallistos (Bishop), "The Transfiguration of the Body," in A.M. Allchin (ed.), *Sacrament and Image*, second edition, London 1987, pp. 19-35.

Whitehead, A.N., *Science and the Modern World*, New York 1926.

Yannaras, Ch., (ed.), *Peri Ylis kai Technis*, Athens 1971.

———— *I Metaphysiki tou Somatos*, Athens 1971.

———— *To Prosopo kai o Eros* [The Person and Eros], Athens 1976.

———— *Elements of Faith: An Introduction to Orthodox Theology*, Edinburgh 1991.

Yioultsis, B.T., *Pnevmatikotita kai koinoniki zoi*, Thessaloniki 1978.

Zizioulas, John (Metropolitan), *I enotis tis Ekklesias en ti theia Efcharistia kai en to episkopo kata tous treis protous aionas*, Athens 1965 (= *Church, Eucharist, Bishop*, Brookline, forthcoming).